NEW TESTAMENT CHRISTIANITY

By J. B. Phillips

THE GOSPELS
translated into Modern English

THE YOUNG CHURCH IN ACTION
A *translation of The Acts of the Apostles*

LETTERS TO YOUNG CHURCHES
A *translation of the New Testament Epistles*

YOUR GOD IS TOO SMALL

MAKING MEN WHOLE

PLAIN CHRISTIANITY *and other broadcast talks*

APPOINTMENT WITH GOD

NEW TESTAMENT CHRISTIANITY

NEW TESTAMENT CHRISTIANITY

by

J. B. Phillips

THE MACMILLAN COMPANY
New York, 1956

Contents

NEW TESTAMENT CHRISTIANITY

Explanation

New Testament Christianity—The critic will probably ask, as he picks up this book, "Is this an attempt to distill the teaching of those early Christian documents which we call the New Testament, or is it an attempt to contrast the vigorous and vivid life of the Young Church with the frequently over-organized and sometimes labored movement of the Church today?" The critic may well feel dubious as to whether there is such a definite phenomenon as "New Testament Christianity" at all, since evidence of life in the early Church is somewhat scanty. He may further reflect that all the major divisions which so sadly separate the world-wide Church owe their divergence of opinion almost entirely to their interpretations of this same New Testament. He may therefore conclude that the author of this book, in writing of "New Testament Christianity," is describing something which may never have had any real coherent existence. He may also feel that it is most unfair to compare the concentrated vigor of a small, newly formed sect with a world-wide organization confronted by problems on a scale unknown to the Young Church and harried by tensions and pressures which could only have existed nineteen hundred years ago in a much simplified form.

Since there is some truth in what this imaginary critic

is feeling, I feel there must be an Explanation at the beginning of this book. I fear that the Explanation must of necessity be somewhat lengthy, but I trust that the reader will read it patiently, for it is necessary for the understanding of the burden of the book.

First, I think I may fairly claim that as a translator of all the New Testament (except the book of Revelation) I am in a somewhat unique position. I do not in the least mean that I am a unique person, and indeed most of my own work of translation has been carried out not in the seclusion of a scholar's study, but in the middle of the busy life of a Church of England Vicar. But I am in an unusual position, for not very many people have lived in close contact with the Greek of the New Testament for some fourteen years. The translator is bound to feel the enormous spiritual energy, indeed, in its truest sense, the inspiration of the Gospels, the Acts and the Epistles. It is not, to speak personally, that particular doctrines, or the seeds of particular dogmas, strike the mind afresh. On the contrary, it is the sheer spiritual zest and drive of the New Testament which fills one with both wonder and wistfulness. It is as though in these pages there lies the secret of human life. The secret is not a mere theory or ideal, but a fresh quality of living worked out in terms of ordinary human life and circumstance. Above all, the general impression is of something supernatural, of suprahuman truth and a suprahuman way of living. The wistfulness arises, of course, from the comparison between the shining, blazing certainty of the New Testament writers and the comparatively tentative and uncertain faith and hope we meet so often in present-day Christianity.

Let me explain this impression of suprahuman quality in more detail. In translating the Gospels, for example, like every other conscientious modern translator, I emptied my mind as far as possible of preconceived ideas and conclusions. "Here," I said to myself in effect, "are four pieces of Greek, comparatively simple Greek, which it is my job to turn into the sort of English which is spoken and written today." I did my best to be detached and disinterested, for it is no part of a translator's job to add color or give a slant to what he is translating. Yet I find on comparing notes with other translators that I am not alone in finding a minor miracle happening. As the work went on, steadily and inexorably there stood up from these pages a Figure of far more than human stature and quality. One tried to sense and indeed to transmit something of the difference in the style of the four evangelists. Mark wrote in a downright "utility" style with neither frills nor decoration, and certainly with a minimum of descriptive adjectives. Matthew's Gospel is careful and precise, a conscientious and, in a sense, calculated short history to prove to the Jewish mind that the One of Whom the prophets foretold was now a Fact of History. Luke (to whose careful research we owe such unforgettable parables as that of the Prodigal Son and the Good Samaritan, as well as the account of the Walk to Emmaus) writes with warm humanity. He is concerned for the Gentile, for the outcast and unprivileged, for the poor, and for the then largely despised female sex. The Gospel of John, written in all probability much later, adds fresh insight, supplying almost another dimension to the Figure simply portrayed by the first three evangelists. Very naturally a composite portrait forms in the mind after many months' study of these four remarkable compositions. But to the present translator it is by no means only the Figure that they succeed in creating between them that is so impressive. The feeling grows that behind these early attempts to set down what was reliably remembered about this Man there stands the Man Himself! It is His Presence, His Character which springs to life at the stimulation of these artless pages. Matthew, Mark, Luke, and John are nothing but humble instruments (as I am sure they would have been the first to admit), *but Who is it, Whose human life is it they are trying to describe and record?* The translator, for all his assumed detachment and impartiality, has all his intuitive and imaginative faculties set at their most sensitive, or his work would be wooden and mechanical. And it is these very faculties which are set tingling and vibrating by the Presence of Someone Who is almost unbearably near and alive today. That He was properly and thoroughly human is obvious from the records; indeed, He is seen to be more human than one thought, for the solemn majesty of the Authorized Version frequently obscures both His humanity and His humor. But steadily there grows in the mind the disquieting conviction that here is much more than man. Here, through the incomplete and sometimes almost naïve records, one is in contact with something so tremendous in its significance that at first the mind cannot grasp it, but only, as it were, gasps incredulously. Previously one had accepted the teaching of the Church's Creeds—that Jesus was both Man and God, and to say one believed in the "Incarnation" would not raise an eyebrow anywhere. But now from first-hand acquaintance with these early documents the truth sweeps in afresh and the indescribable humility of God strikes one with overwhelming awe. This little sphere on which we live and move and have our being is in fact a *Visited Planet.* The Creator of the vast Universe, about Whose Nature we could at the most make intelligent guesses, slipped quietly into the stream of human life in the only way in which that could be possible, by becoming a human being. This is the truth that pulses and vibrates behind the steady prose of Matthew, Mark, and Luke and shines through the more poetic works of John.

It now becomes apparent why, though the work of translating must be done as conscientiously as possible, the translator constantly feels not merely his own inadequacy but the extreme difficulty of his task. For behind all that he translates is not simply a uniquely important event of history, though that would be a profound understatement; not simply the story of the greatest man who ever lived, though that again would fall a long way below the truth, but the active Presence of God Himself, God expressed in a form human beings can understand, in a form that can bring both inestimable comfort and surprising disquiet. This astonishing sense of spiritual attack which, it seems to me, must inevitably follow the continual reading of the four Gospels, without preconception but with an alert mind, is not the sole privilege of the translator. It can happen to anyone who is prepared to abandon proof texts and a closed attitude of mind and allow not merely the stories, but the quality of the Figure Who exists behind the stories to meet him afresh. Neat snippets of a few verses are of course useful in their way, but the over-all sweep and much of the significance of the Gospel narratives are lost to us unless we are prepared to read the Gospels through, not once but several times. I would suggest that this be done in an unfamiliar version, not of course necessarily my own! Familiar words and verses have already their stereotyped reactions. It is not the significance of a single verse that we are seeking here —though Heaven knows there are enough single verses to revolutionize our thinking—so much as the full meaning that lies behind the total narrative. From countless conversations and from a good deal of correspondence, I have become convinced that very few present-day Christians have allowed the Truth to break over them in this way. What is more, I have a feeling, although it cannot be proved, that most of the critics of the Christian religion have never given their serious adult attention to the Gospel records. It is easy to criticize the many failings of the Church; it is all too easy to criticize the lives of those who profess and call themselves Christians; but I should say that it is almost impossible to read the Gospels thoroughly with adult serious attention and then dismiss the central Figure as a mere human prophet or tragic idealist. The reaction to such study may indeed prove to be either conversion or open hostility, but it would at least mean the end of childish and ill informed attacks upon what is supposed to be the Christian religion.

The total impression, then, of the close study of the Gospels is an indelible conviction that the well-nigh incredible has happened—that the Creator has visited this world in human form. He brings with Him confirmation of our highest hopes; He endorses our finest longings; and He confirms many of our intuitions. But of course He does far more than this. First, He introduces a new kind of truth—a kind of "supersense" which transcends our earthly viewpoint. We may find sometimes our values disconcertingly reversed; sometimes we find we have been looking at things from the wrong angle. Now that we have this revelation of truth, there is no need to grope or fumble. We have certain basic truths unquestionably revealed. We have a standard by which our scale of values and our conscience may be adjusted. It is not that all our questions are immediately answered. It is not that everything becomes immediately plain and that there are no more mysteries. But it is true that we now have enough light by which to live; we see something at least of life's point and purpose, and we know where we are going. What is more, the humble and obedient are guaranteed an active, energetic, contemporary Spirit of truth. In other words, although we see the Character of God focused historically in the time-and-space setup, we come to see and know that that human appearance is only the outcrop of what is eternally true. (That is why the material on which a New Testament translator works is alive under his hands.) It is almost too good to be true, but it *is* true, that the One Who walked and talked in the countryside, in the streets and houses of Palestine nearly two thousand years ago, is in every way as alive and active in the world of today.

The second important revelation which God-become-Man gave us, and which indeed His Spirit is continually prepared to endorse, is that this little life is lived against a background, at present invisible, of timeless Reality. Some men have always felt that this must be so, since man's longings and intuitions, as well as his sense of justice, go far beyond the limits of life in this present temporary existence. To put it in another way, there is another dimension to life altogether, the dimension of "eternity." This present life is interpenetrated by the Real World far more than we know. For most of us it is only very occasionally that we get our flashes of conviction, and it is of immeasurable comfort to know, on the authority of that Personal Visit, that our feeble intuition was right and that this short earthly life, important and significant though it may be in its setting, is no more than a prelude to a share in the timeless Life of God.

All this and much more floods our minds as we study afresh the four Gospel records. But this wonderful quality of living, this drawing on unseen spiritual resources, this plunging of the sharp sword of truth into the muddle of human sins and stupidities might have ended with the crucifixion of Jesus. If it had, we should indeed have been left something, for every true seer and poet and philosopher has left us the richer. But the special glory of the New Testament is that we are not merely shown a shining beacon of one perfect human life, but we are told of what happened after that human life was ended. The light persists; the power continues; the wind of Heaven does not cease to blow. If you will not misunderstand me, in one sense I have been even more thrilled as a translator to come into contact with the highly charged material of the Acts and the Epistles than I was when translating the Gospels. For if God really became Man, the light and power and splendor of the Gospel story is only to be expected. But to find that this was not merely a single unique demonstration, but the beginning of a new way of living, the founding of a new Kingdom and of a new fellowship, is exciting indeed!

Consequently the close study of the book commonly called the Acts of the Apostles proved an exhilaration. The ideas and ideals of God-become-Man take shape and form. The glory has not departed; it continues and expands. For the first time in human history we are seeing a group of men and women united in devotion to the unseen King, joined in an unconquerable fellowship. We may be reasonably certain that Luke was a most careful historian and was not prone to exaggeration. Yet we find his story of the Young Church in action bearing the same stamp of suprahuman quality which we find in the Gospels. The sick are not merely prayed about; they are healed, often suddenly and dramatically. Mental and psychological diseases ("possession by evil spirits," in the jargon of those days) proved equally susceptible to the new power in the Church. Perhaps above all, that miracle which is theoretically unattainable is performed again and again—human nature is changed. The fresh air of Heaven blows gustily through these pages, and the sense that ordinary human life is continually open to the Spirit of God is very marked. There is not yet a dead hand of tradition; there is no over-organization to stifle initiative; there is neither security nor complacency to destroy sensitivity to the living God. The early Church lived dangerously, but never before has such a handful of people exerted such widespread influence. There is a courage to match the vision; there is a flexible willingness to match the divine leadership. And there is that unshakable certainty against which persecution, imprisonment, and death prove quite powerless. To put it shortly and in the common phrase, the lasting excitement which follows the reading of this book is this: *The thing works!* What might have remained no more than a beautiful ideal is set to work in an actual human situation, and with truly astonishing impetus the Church moves forward on its way.

All this is without doubt exciting enough, but from the point of view of Christian evidence the best is yet to be. For, after all, it might be argued, and indeed has been argued, that the Man Jesus did exist but that some years after His death, perhaps after a generation or so, His followers wrote romantic and idealistic accounts of His life. Again, it is possible to argue that Luke's second book, the Acts of the Apostles, is something of an idealization of the beginnings of the Christian Church. But even if these contentions are true, if both the Gospels and the Acts were propaganda for the Christian sect and therefore not to be wholly relied upon as unbiased history, the critics of Christianity have still to explain the incontrovertible evidence of the "Epistles" or Letters. With one or two minor exceptions these are universally accepted as authentic, and it seems to me that Christians today do not always realize how valuable they are as evidence for the proof of the Faith. For here we have no self-conscious documents, but vivid human letters, often bearing strong evidence of the emotion under which they were written. There is some case to be made out for arguing that the four evangelists knew what they were doing; they were writing lives of Jesus Christ to be read among Christians and possibly non-Christians. Although they could not have foreseen the vast weight of authority that would later be accorded to their words, they may well have known that they were in a sense writing "holy Scripture." But this is not true of Paul, for example, at all. For the most part he wrote to certain groups of Christians in certain circumstances, and he had no idea that he was writing holy Scripture at the time. In translating his letters it is not difficult to picture that solitary, courageous figure writing or dictating his letters in great haste and urgency. Sometimes he was in prison; sometimes he was in poor health; frequently he was torn with anxiety for his newborn converts. He wrote to meet the needs of those for whom he was writing, completely unconscious that in years to come millions of people would study his every word with the deepest attention. Yet the inspiration of his words, which I believe to be largely unconscious, strikes us forcibly today. He had no idea, certainly, that he was composing Christian evidence! Yet the life reflected, as well as expressed, in the pages of his unselfconscious letters is plainly of the suprahuman quality.

Now if we were to compile a history of any place or nation, one of our most valuable discoveries would be a packet of letters reflecting the life of a certain part of that history. Newspapers, broadsheets, pamphlets, and any other printed matter would have their value of course; but because they were written for the public eye, and probably to prove a particular point, we should be very wary of accepting them as unbiased evidence. But that would not be true of a bundle of private letters, simply because they were not being written for the public at all, and the writer had no particular ax to grind. They would in all probability reflect most accurately the customs, habits, and thoughts of the times in which they were written. Now if this is true in the field of purely secular history, it is just as true, though of far deeper significance, when we study historically the beginnings of Christianity. What the Letters say and what the Letters imply, the new-quality life revealed by these human unselfconscious documents, give us, to my mind, our most valuable Christian evidence. What impression is left upon our minds, or, if I may again be personal, what impression is left upon my mind after spending some years in translating these letters? Above all, I think, that men and women are being changed: the timid become brave; the filthy-minded become pure in heart; the mean and selfish become loving and generous. It is quite plain that the writers of these letters took it as a matter of course, as a matter of observed experience, that if men and women were open to the Spirit of God, then they could be and were transformed. The resources of God are not referred to as vague pieties, but as readily available spiritual power. Quite clearly a positive torrent of love and wisdom, sanity and courage has already flooded human life, and is always ready to flow wherever human hearts are open.

Now critics of Christianity have somehow got to explain this if they are to have a leg to stand on. Let them read these Letters for themselves and attempt to explain these transformations of character. No one had anything to gain in those days from being a Christian; indeed, there was a strong chance that the Christian would lose security and property and even life itself. Yet, reflected in the pages of these Letters, both men and women are exhibiting superb courage and are growing, as naturally as fruit upon a tree, those qualities of the spirit of which the world is so lamentably short. To my mind we are forced to the conclusion that something is at work here far above and beyond normal human experience, which can only be explained if we accept what the New Testament itself claims, that is, that ordinary men and women had become, through the power of Christ, sons and daughters of God.

With all this lengthy, but I think necessary, preamble, I now come to define my use of the term "New Testament Christianity." I am not in the least concerned with what may or may not be proved by the dexterous manipulation of texts. Indeed, I think we are all of us indoctrinated more than we know by being led tendentiously from one text to another in our impressionable years. But I am concerned with this new quality of living which has as its spearhead the personal visit of God to this planet in the Person of Jesus Christ. It does not, thank God, exist only in these pages or in the lives reflected in these pages. It exists today, and I myself have seen it in people of all ages and of many different occupations. It has been my privilege to mix freely among many denominations, and I can truthfully report that I have found New Testament Christians exhibiting the same stamp of suprahuman quality in them all. What is even more important is that I have found something very like this first century fellowship among Christians of widely differing nationalities. There are the same essentials of New Testament Christianity to be found in men and women whatever the color of their skin, and for the fact that I have observed this I am profoundly thankful.

It has been my privilege during the last few years to preach, lecture, and generally join in the fellowship of churches, both in this country and for a few weeks in the United States. I have mostly been asked to speak about the New Testament and its translation, and that has invariably led on to the discussion of what we mean by "New Testament Christianity"—its distinguishing marks, its qualities and its roots. I have been enormously heartened by the fact that there are thousands of people who are sick of narrowness and churchiness, and who long for the fresh air of the New Testament. I am greatly encouraged too by the obvious fact that thousands of people deplore the spiritual loss that the Church has plainly sustained since the days of Pentecost. There is, I find, a hunger, sometimes almost a desperate hunger, to regain the shining certainties and revel in the freedom and power of the newborn Church. My own experience is necessarily small, but I am firmly of the opinion that so great is the longing for New Testament Christianity that it will be along this line that true spiritual revival will come.

The Angels' Point of View

On Palm Sunday many of us sing a hymn containing these lines:

> The Angel armies of the skies
> Look down with sad and wondering eyes
> To see the approaching Sacrifice.

That of course is "only a hymn," but we have at least one piece of evidence from the Gospels that the angels of God are interested in human affairs. For Jesus Himself said, "I tell you there is joy among the angels in Heaven over one sinner that repenteth." [1] If then there is joy, why should there not be sorrow? And why indeed should not those other beings which God has created, different though they may be from ourselves, watch the unfolding of the human drama with the deepest interest? These celestial beings live, as far as we know, perpetually in the Royal Presence. Apart from the fact that they are sometimes used as messengers, seen or unseen, from that world to this, we know nothing of the reasons for their existence. Nevertheless, it helps sometimes to break in imagination the fetters of earth and try to see things from the angels' point of view. We might even go so far as to say that this is part

[1] Luke 15:10.

14

of Paul's thought when he talks of it being possible to "sit together with Christ." [2]

It may give us a fresh perspective on life, if for a few moments we shed the limitations of earthbound thinking, and detach ourselves deliberately from modern pressures and problems. Let us pretend for a little while; the pretense may be fanciful, but it may help us to let the real truth break over us afresh.

*   *   *

Once upon a time a very young angel was being shown round the splendors and glories of the universes by a senior and experienced angel. To tell the truth, the little angel was beginning to be tired and a little bored. He had been shown whirling galaxies and blazing suns, infinite distances in the deathly cold of interstellar space, and to his mind there seemed to be an awful lot of it all. Finally he was shown the galaxy of which our planetary system is but a small part. As the two of them drew near to the star which we call our sun and to its circling planets, the senior angel pointed to a small and rather insignificant sphere turning very slowly on its axis. It looked as dull as a dirty tennis ball to the little angel whose mind was filled with the size and glory of what he had seen.

"I want you to watch that one particularly," said the senior angel, pointing with his finger.

"Well, it looks very small and rather dirty to me," said the little angel. "What's special about that one?"

"That," replied his senior solemnly, "is the Visited Planet."

" 'Visited'?" said the little one. "You don't mean visited by—"

[2] Ephesians 2:6.

"*Indeed I do. That ball, which I have no doubt looks to you small and insignificant and not perhaps overclean, has been visited by our young Prince of Glory.*" And at these words he bowed his head reverently.

"*But how?*" queried the younger one. "*Do you mean that our great and glorious Prince, with all these wonders and splendors of His Creation, and millions more that I'm sure I haven't seen yet, went down in Person to this fifth-rate little ball? Why should He do a thing like that?*"

"*It isn't for us,*" said his senior, a little stiffly, "*to question His 'why's,' except that I must point out to you that He is not impressed by size and numbers as you seem to be. But that He really went I know, and all of us in Heaven who know anything know that. As to why He became one of them . . . How else do you suppose could He visit them?*"

The little angel's face wrinkled in disgust.

"*Do you mean to tell me,*" he said, "*that He stooped so low as to become one of those creeping, crawling creatures of that floating ball?*"

"*I do, and I don't think He would like you to call them 'creeping crawling creatures' in that tone of voice. For, strange as it may seem to us, He loves them. He went down to visit them to lift them up to become like Him.*"

The little angel looked blank. Such a thought was almost beyond his comprehension.

"*Close your eyes for a moment,*" said the senior angel, "*and we will go back in what they call Time.*"

While the little angel's eyes were closed and the two of them moved nearer to the spinning ball, it stopped its spinning, spun backward quite fast for a while, and then slowly resumed its usual rotation.

"*Now look!*" and as the little angel did as he was told, there appeared here and there on the dull surface of the *globe little flashes of light, some merely momentary and some persisting for quite a time.*

"Well, what am I seeing now?" queried the little angel.

"You are watching this little world as it was some thousands of years ago," returned his companion. "Every flash and glow of light that you see is something of the Father's knowledge and wisdom breaking into the minds and hearts of people who live upon the earth. Not many people, you see, can hear His Voice or understand what He says, even though He is speaking gently and quietly to them all the time."

"Why are they so blind and deaf and stupid?" asked the junior angel rather crossly.

"It is not for us to judge them. We who live in the Splendor have no idea what it is like to live in the dark. We hear the music and the Voice like the sound of many waters every day of our lives, but to them—well, there is much darkness and much noise and much distraction upon the earth. Only a few who are quiet and humble and wise hear His Voice. But watch, for in a moment you will see something truly wonderful."

The Earth went on turning and circling round the sun, and then, quite suddenly, in the upper half of the globe there appeared a light, tiny, but so bright in its intensity that both the angels hid their eyes.

"I think I can guess," said the little angel in a low voice. "That was the Visit, wasn't it?"

"Yes, that was the Visit. The Light Himself went down there and lived among them; but in a moment, and you will be able to tell that even with your eyes closed, the light will go out."

"But why? Could He not bear their darkness and stupidity? Did He have to return here?"

"No, it wasn't that," returned the senior angel. His

voice was stern and sad. "They failed to recognize Him for Who He was—or at least only a handful knew Him. For the most part they preferred their darkness to His Light, and in the end they killed Him."

"The fools, the crazy fools! They don't deserve—"

"Neither you nor I nor any other angel knows why they were so foolish and so wicked. Nor can we say what they deserve or don't deserve. But the fact remains, they killed our Prince of Glory while He was Man amongst them."

"And that, I suppose, was the end? I see the whole Earth has gone black and dark. All right, I won't judge them, but surely that is all they could expect?"

"Wait. We are still far from the end of the story of the Visited Planet. Watch now, but be ready to cover your eyes again."

In utter blackness the Earth turned round three times, and then there blazed with unbearable radiance a point of light.

"What now?" asked the little angel shielding his eyes.

"They killed Him, all right, but He conquered death. The thing most of them dread and fear all their lives He broke and conquered. He rose again, and a few of them saw Him, and from then on became His utterly devoted slaves."

"Thank God for that!" said the little angel.

"Amen. Open your eyes now; the dazzling light has gone. The Prince has returned to His Home of Light. But watch the Earth now."

As they looked, in place of the dazzling light there was a bright glow which throbbed and pulsated. And then as the Earth turned many times, little points of light spread out. A few flickered and died, but for the most part the lights burned steadily, and as they continued to watch, in *many parts of the globe there was a glow over many areas.*

"You see what is happening?" asked the senior angel. "The bright glow is the company of loyal men and women He left behind, and with His help they spread the glow, and now lights begin to shine all over the Earth."

"Yes, yes," said the little angel impatiently. "But how does it end? Will the little lights join up with one another? Will it all be light, as it is in Heaven?"

His senior shook his head. "We simply do not know," he replied. "It is in the Father's hands. Sometimes it is agony to watch, and sometimes it is joy unspeakable. The end is not yet. But now I am sure you can see why this little ball is so important. He has visited it; He is working out His Plan upon it."

"Yes, I see, though I don't understand. I shall never forget that this is the Visited Planet. . . ."

*   *   *

Imaginary? Fanciful? Certainly, but a good deal truer than some of our current modern thinking. For in the eyes of the Eternal World this little planet is of the highest importance simply because it is the Visited Planet. We may not realize it at all, but we are right plumb in the middle of a vast drama, a tremendous battle between light and darkness. The whole core and essence of the Christian Faith, which many of us hold so lightly, is that Light Himself visited our darkness, scaled down to fit the human scene. It is true that since the Visit we know for certain that this rolling ball is by no means our permanent home; our destiny is higher even than that of the angels. But today, and every day that we live in the here-and-now, we are part of the vast Experiment, the age-long Battle, whose stage and testing ground is the planet which we call the Earth.

God Makes News

That this is a Visited Planet was the heart and core of the Young Church's faith. Many of the very early Christians had of course actually seen the young Prince of Glory during His earthly life. They had by no means always known Who He was, but after the resounding demonstration of the Resurrection, and after the unforgettable reassurances of His appearing and disappearing thereafter, they knew beyond any doubt that the Visit had taken place. Since almost all the early Christians were Jews, the fact which they had observed fitted, after their initial incredulity, into the pattern of their thinking. The Old Testament Scriptures which they knew so well foretold again and again the Personal Visit. The "Greater Prophet," the "Holy One," the "Righteous Servant," and all the other hints and previsions had come true in Jesus of Nazareth. They went out with gay and unconquerable courage to declare that the hope of Israel had come true: Jesus was indeed the Christ of God. It was not long before they saw that the Hope of Israel was also the Hope of the world, and that the Visit was not merely the fulfillment of a promise to a chosen nation but the coming into the world of "the light that lighteth every man." [1] Therefore, they preached Good News, the Good News that men were no

[1] John 1:9.

longer fumbling and groping after God in the darkness. He had focused Himself in a Person, the Man Jesus, and by faith in this Man men could begin to live.

Naturally, as the message spread and as time went on, the number of those who had known the Son of God personally grew relatively few. But even though the new converts in their thousands believed by faith and not by sight, yet the central fact remained the same—God had paid His Visit. From now on, the center of changed lives, the heart of new loyalties, was Jesus Christ Who was both God and Man.

If New Testament Christianity is to reappear today with its power and joy and courage, men must recapture the basic conviction that this is a Visited Planet. It is not enough to express formal belief in the "Incarnation" or in the "Divinity of Christ"; the staggering truth must be accepted afresh that in this vast mysterious Universe, of which we are an almost infinitesimal part, the great Mystery, Whom we call God, has visited our planet in Person. It is from this conviction that there spring unconquerable certainty and unquenchable faith and hope. It is not enough to believe theoretically that Jesus was both God and Man; not enough to admire, respect, and even worship Him; it is not even enough to try to follow Him. The reason for the insufficiency of these things is that the modern intelligent mind, which has had its horizons widened in dozens of different ways, has got to be shocked afresh by the audacious central Fact that as a sober matter of history *God became one of us*.

This primary Fact is the foundation of all New Testament certainty about God and life. But there is a second conviction which is almost equally important. For while it is true that the earliest Christians had personally witnessed the breakthrough of Eternity into time, they did not regard this as a solitary isolated action. The Young Church lived in the daily demonstrable conviction that this world was continually interpenetrated by the world of the Spirit. Indeed, though some of them had seen the Man Jesus ascend into the clouds before their astonished eyes, the fact that He was with them and in them became an increasing joyful certainty. To anyone who studies the book we call the Acts of the Apostles it becomes quite plain that the Holy Spirit is not a vague influence for good, not even just a powerful Wind of Heaven, but a Person with a purpose and ideas of His own. The earth was once visited for a few years, visibly, audibly, and tangibly by God in human form, but thereafter it was (and, of course, is) continually subject to invasions by the Spirit of Jesus. Happily, the Young Church was sensitive, alert, and flexible, and we can read for ourselves to what miraculous triumphs the Spirit led them. Again, if we are to regain the buoyant God-consciousness of New Testament Christianity, we must not only accept afresh the planned Personal Visit but be ready for any number of subsequent invasions of the Spirit.

It seems to me that it is well worth our while to study the leading characteristics of New Testament Christians. These men and women, when all is said and done, were as human as we are. God cannot conceivably have changed in His Nature or Purpose over the centuries, but we may find, as we compare the life-attitude of New Testament Christians with our own, that a subtle but disastrous change has come over us in the intervening centuries. We may find that our timidity and rigidity, our prejudices and preconceived ideas, are most effectively blocking the Purpose of God. We must take the risk of being wide open on the God-ward side.

The Faith Faculty

Quite a number of present-day Christians are consciously or unconsciously on the defensive. They are only too well aware that they are a small minority, and many of them are faithfully and strenuously defending their convictions. Their courage and loyalty to Christ in the face of the widespread apathy of the surrounding world is wholly admirable. But, with some notable exceptions, the Christian Faith is only being maintained within existing churches and is not spreading very far beyond actual church membership. However much we love the Church, we have to admit that though it may exhibit the quieter and more inconspicuous virtues, it is very rarely making any considerable impact upon the modern pattern of living. It has unquestionably lost power, and it has lost vision; while in the worst cases the Christian Faith itself is being reduced to a dreary duty performance which, to say the least of it, is most unattractive.

No doubt there are many reasons for the deterioration in quality in Christian faith and Christian living over the centuries, but one explanation which I personally regard as wholly inadmissible is to blame the passage of time, that is, our distance measured in years from the events recorded in the New Testament. I regard this as inadmissible partly because of the Nature of God, which is naturally unchangeable, and partly because I cannot believe Jesus Christ founded a Church which was intended to taper off into ineffective mediocrity. Further, it is only too easy for many present-day Christians to owe their loyalty to the present-day Church, and be content as long as they are keeping the minimal rules of conduct prescribed. They are forgetting the awe-inspiring contemporaneousness of God, and that their own church, though still living, may have become senile through failing to renew its youth by open contact with the living God. This safe, limited loyalty makes the power and glory of invasion by the divine quality of living almost impossible.

Even more than the limiting and inhibiting effects of our preconceived loyalties is the mental climate of our age, which affects all of us, whether Christians or not, far more than we know. We have become conditioned to regarding this earthly life of ours as a completely closed system of cause and effect. Because Science has made such enormous strides and can explain to our satisfaction so much of the physical world, and thus offers intelligent explanations of what was previously sheer mystery, we are inclined to forget that Science at its apparently most omniscient is only dealing with one particular stratum or aspect of Truth. Again, modern psychology has made enormous strides in the understanding and explanation of human behavior. But while it throws a great deal of light on what was previously dark (and has, we hope, much more light to shed), we need to remember that the psychologist also is dealing only with certain aspects of Truth —in this case emotional and mental life. We should be foolish to disregard this new knowledge, but we should be still more foolish if we thought that by means of physical and mental science the whole of life can now be accounted for. It seems to me that we are missing a dimension in our thinking which we may call for the moment the dimension of God. It was awareness of this dimension which produced the startling vigor and unassailable certainty of the Young Church.

In this modern age, which treats as commonplace that which our grandparents would have thought miraculous, we ought to be able to grasp numerous analogies to help us understand how several media or dimensions can co-exist. Let us select one very obvious but useful example from our common modern life. As I write these words I am aware of various things through my physical senses. As it happens, at the moment these are chiefly the light and warmth of sunshine, the beauty of trees in full leaf, the varied songs of birds and the distant sound of children at play. I am also mentally aware of the truth I am trying to express, and of you, my imaginary reader, following the line of thought I am trying to make clear. Doubtless as you read you are taking in similar sense impressions, as well as having your thoughts guided by the complicated system of marks made upon paper which we call printing. But simultaneously, in the immediate world of you the reader and me the writer, there are radio programs of various kinds actually in our rooms with us. The "ether" (for that is the name given to this all-pervasive but intangible medium) is continually pulsing and vibrating, strongly or feebly, with perhaps a hundred or more near or distant radio transmissions. In common parlance we frequently say that a certain program is "on the air"; but that, of course, is quite inaccurate. Radio transmissions are not vibrations in the air. They would function just as well if there were no air at all, and they make their way, as we all know, with very little hindrance through such things as timber, stone, and concrete. It is only when they meet conductors or partial conductors of electricity that these inaudible, invisible vibrations become minute electric currents, and even then they are undetectable except by that commonplace but quite complicated piece of circuitry known as a radio set. In your body, as in my body, there are at this very moment minute electrical currents of which we are quite unaware. They are, in fact, an untuned jumble of electrical vibrations representing the assorted offerings of many radio transmissions. Now we are unaware of this and normally we take no notice of it. It is only when we want to hear a particular radio program that we tune in a certain band of these etheric vibrations and by means of the radio set turn them back into audible sound. For even if we disapprove of radio, even if we refuse to believe in its all-pervasive presence, it makes not the slightest difference to the *fact*. Whether we like it or not, or whether we believe it or not, we are permeated by this mysterious "ether," and that is a fact which can easily be demonstrated. Before the advent of radio less than a century ago, such an idea would have seemed in the highest degree improbable and even impossible. We know today that it is true; that simultaneously with our ordinary-world sense impressions there coexists a world of mysterious "ether" of which we only become aware when certain apparatus is used.

Now, this seems to me a most helpful, if simple, analogy. Suppose it is possible that the whole material world and the whole psychological world are interpenetrated by what we may call the "spiritual." For some reason or other we are inclined to think of the physical world and even the demonstrable world of the "ether" as somehow real, while the "spiritual" is regarded as unreal and imaginary. I believe the opposite to be true. As Paul foresaw long ago, "The things which are seen are temporal; but the things which are not seen are eternal." [1] Suppose what we are seeing and measuring and observing are the outward expressions in the time and space setup of what is really eternal and spiritual! If we make such a supposition we are in for a revolution in our whole way of thinking. But New Testament Christians had already experienced this revolution.

To sense the reality of the God-dimension, to conform to its purpose and order, to perceive its working in and through the visible world system, is, speaking broadly, what the Bible calls faith. The heroes of Old Testament days were invariably the men, and in some cases the women, who exercised their faculty of faith even when it appeared to contradict the evidence of their five senses. In those old days the king, the prophet, the priest, the warrior sensed intuitively what has today become very largely a missing dimension. There is much in the Old Testament which may strike us as outmoded and even tedious, but its particular genius is to point to and record the actions of those people who were, however dimly, living life with a consciousness of the Eternal Order.

Naturally, when we come to the pages of the New Testament, we find this faculty vastly enhanced. For those fortunate enough to see and know God in the Person of Jesus Christ the human being, and recognize Who He was, the faculty of faith was naturally stimulated and confirmed. Peter, for example, blurts out a truth which others besides himself must have been thinking when he exclaims, "Thou hast the words of eternal life." [2] He means surely that the truth of Christ's teaching is to be recognized as part of the permanent Order. In this exclamation and in his even more famous one, "Thou art the Christ, the Son of the living God," [3] Peter is saying that the very focal

[1] 2 Corinthians 4:18.   [2] John 6:68.   [3] Matthew 16:16.

point of faith is alive before them; the heart and center of the unseen eternal dimension has broken into the time and space setup in visible form.

It is easy for us to think how slow Christ's contemporaries were to recognize Him. But in an extraordinary way it was particularly difficult. For the best of men faith means believing in the dark, believing sometimes in spite of ordinary evidences and proofs. It was not easy for them, nor would it be for us, to realize that the unique and unforeseeable had happened—that the King of the very order which they grasped so dimly was living and present before their eyes. It was not really until after the Resurrection that they dared to believe what seemed too good to be true. But thereafter thousands upon thousands began to live their lives from the new heavenly point of view by putting their faith in the focused God, Jesus Christ.

In a way it is a pity that we have to use the word "faith" to describe the faculty by which the unseen dimension is grasped, drawn upon, and lived by. It is only a pity because to many of us, if we are honest, "faith" has degenerated into a rather dogged holding on to something which we believe to be true. Of course, ideas of belief and personal trust are involved in what the New Testament calls faith. Nevertheless, it might help us to grasp the truth afresh if we saw it as a faculty as real as seeing or hearing, thinking or feeling. Suppose it is true, as I am sure it is, that we are at all times surrounded and permeated by this "spiritual" dimension. Suppose, too, that we need the x faculty in order to appreciate this further dimension. Can we not see that it is the x faculty which has deteriorated over the centuries between us and the Church's young days? I believe we all have this faculty, but in many of us it has become atrophied almost to vanishing point. Since it is obvious throughout the New Testament that the x faculty is the indispensable link between the resources of the unseen world and this temporary one, we can easily understand how the serious falling off in the use and practice of "faith" throughout the Church at large has resulted in a marked loss of spiritual power.

It would appear that one of the great reasons for our living on this planet at all is that we may learn to use and develop this faculty. As the author of the Epistle to the Hebrews succinctly puts it, "Without faith it is impossible to please him," [4] which simply means that if we do not use our faith faculty we are bound to be out of harmony with the divine Plan. Why this should be so we simply do not know, but it is one of the primary facts which we have to accept.

Obviously it is much easier merely to use our ordinary physical and mental faculties. The whole pattern of the world's life disregards, for the most part, the existence of this faith faculty and its practical application to the business of living. Once we begin to use it we shall find a certain opposition in the ordinary earthbound pattern of thinking by which we are surrounded. We shall also find in ourselves a certain reluctance comparable to the physical pain we experience in bringing into play a long-disused muscle. But the effort must be made, the initial stiffness overcome, if we are to use again the vital faculty which gives point and quality to life.

The Faith Faculty in the New Testament

If we look at the New Testament records with an eye to seeing how this faculty was stimulated and developed, we may be surprised to find how essential it is. Both in

[4] Hebrews 11:6.

the Gospels and in the Letters it is the use of this faculty which makes life of a new quality possible. It is obviously out of the question to examine here every reference to the word "faith," but I shall suggest a few instances which may open up profitable lines of thinking.

In the Gospels it would appear in general that the existence and use of this faculty provided the link between the Divine Order and human life. The centurion who earned Jesus' commendation for his "faith" plainly took it as a matter of course that as he occupied a position of authority in the purely earthly realm, so Jesus was able to exercise authority in the unseen realm.[5] It was not so much personal admiration for Jesus, and probably not full recognition of Who He really was, so much as an intuitive perception that here was One Who was a Master over the unseen forces which influence observed life. His "faith" was nevertheless a sincere recognition that there was a Divine Order which was real and reliable. Again, in the case of those four young men who were prepared to take desperate measures to get their friend to Jesus, there was the same recognition of the unseen Divine Order and Power.[6] In both these cases, and of course in many others, the use of the faith faculty was, so to speak, the agent which enabled Jesus' power to be released. The contrary was also true. Where men were imprisoned by the closed system and could not, for reasons of prejudice or sheer unwillingness to believe, break through into the real dimension, even the power of Jesus was inhibited. In Nazareth "He could do no mighty works there because of their unbelief." [7] We read moreover that "he marvelled because of their unbelief," [8] and surely we may fairly guess that His observation of men's failure to use their faculty of

[5] Matthew 8:5; Luke 7:2.   [7] Matthew 13:58.
[6] Mark 2:3; Luke 5:18.   [9] Mark 6:6.

faith must have continually astonished Him. To Him the
Unseen Dimension and Order were continuously real. The
love, the generosity, and the power of the Father were
constant realities, and it must not only have amazed but
grieved Him more than we can guess to find men either
unwilling or unable to use the power of faith. Again and
again He urges men to "have faith in God," and both by
His own teaching and His own example it is plain that He
is continually urging men to put the weight of their con-
fidence not in earthly schemes and values, but in the unseen Heavenly Order, of which the supreme Head is the
Father. To live like this, to live as though the spiritual
realities were infinitely more important than the appearance of things, might fairly be said to be a basic teaching of Jesus. To live "by faith" is to Him the truly natural
way of living, and although it may demand effort and
persistence He does not hold it out as a way of living
merely for the spiritual élite. It is only in the exceptional
cases, as in the case of the healing of the epileptic boy,[9]
that Jesus declares that training and discipline are necessary for faith to produce the requisite power for good. In
general throughout the Gospels Jesus seems to be urging
men to dare to use their faith faculty—to knock, to seek, to
ask. His general implication is that there are boundless
resources in the Unseen World available for men of faith.

There were, and are, many reasons for man's non-use
of the faith faculty. We shall find it rewarding to study the
Gospel records themselves, and, by using a little imagination, to see the reasons which prevented men from believing even when the Truth was with them in Person.
There is one significant remark of Jesus' which is worth
mentioning here. He said on one occasion, "How can you
believe while you receive honor one from another?" [10]

[9] Luke 9:39.   [10] John 5:44.

This is surely a most important remark, for we may fairly infer from it that in order to "believe" or properly exercise the faith faculty we must be prepared to disregard the honors, commendations, and even values of this passing world. May I suggest that we pause at this point and consider why it is that we ourselves make so little use of the faith faculty? Is it simply laziness, the unwillingness to use an almost atrophied function of our personalities, or are we so bound by the present world system that we cannot "believe"? I am convinced that there will be no recovery of the vitality and vigor of New Testament Christianity until we who call ourselves Christians dare to break through contemporary habits of thought and touch the resources of God.

In the teaching of Jesus the use of the faith faculty does not, of course, only mean recognizing that there is a Divine Order and that there are Divine resources. He frequently made it a far more personal matter than that. He taught that men could live without worry and fear if they would use their faith faculty to realize that the One in charge of the whole mysterious world and indeed of everything, seen or unseen, is man's Heavenly Father. Now this may be believing in spite of appearances, for there is much in this sinful and imperfect world to contradict such an idea. But to Jesus it was the fundamental fact, a fact which once firmly grasped by heart and mind affects a man's life both here and in what we call the "hereafter." Consider His words, "He that heareth my word, and believeth on Him that sent me, *hath* everlasting life." [11] What is this but a plain assurance that if a man accepts the teaching of Christ as the fundamental expression of the Father's authority and plan, he enters already upon that timeless quality of living which is sometimes called

[11] John 5:24.

"eternal life"? In other words, if a man uses his faith faculty to grasp with heart and mind the essential truth about life he becomes part of Real Life. The well known words of Jesus, "According to your faith be it unto you," [12] take on a new meaning if we are thinking of faith not as a desperate effort to believe, so much as the using of a faculty to grasp unseen realities and utilize unseen resources.

"Faith" in the Young Church

When we come to the book of the Acts of the Apostles or the Letters of the New Testament, we are reading about what actually happened when men and women began to "believe in the Lord Jesus Christ." The burden of preaching in the Acts is not, so far as can be discovered, the emphasis on man's depravity, but on faith—the grasping by the faith faculty of the new order. Naturally, the focal point of this new apprehension is God's personal focusing of Himself in the Man Jesus Christ. The word translated "repentance" does not necessarily mean being sorry for our sins, though that will probably be included. *Metanoia* means a fundamental change of outlook. As far as we can discover in the early preaching of the Gospel, the Good News was not primarily the announcement of the fact that men were sinners, but that the real world had broken through into this world in visible, tangible form —in fact, in Christ. God was now knowable; His Plan of a universal Kingdom was manifest; death itself was of no account now that God had revealed Himself in Jesus. Simultaneous with this proclamation of Good News to Jews and Gentiles was the announcement that the living contemporary Spirit of God was alive and active. We have only to read the book of the Acts to see how He, the Holy

[12] Matthew 9:29.

Spirit, the Spirit of Jesus, empowered, transformed, and guided the early Christians. The Young Church was full of divine energy and wisdom; and it would seem that its members were so filled because they learned more and more to use the faculty of faith, and because they prayed, not indeed to persuade an unwilling God, but to bring themselves into line with His Purpose so that the power could safely be given. No one could honestly read the book of the Acts with an adult mind without being impressed with this sense of suprahuman power, wisdom, and authority. God Himself is plainly at work in and through these new Christians who, for all their faults, were plainly exercising the faith faculty.

When we enter the world of the Letters, which reflect the life of the early Church, we are again faced with the phenomenon of people whose whole outlook and pattern of life are being transformed by the use of the same faculty of faith. If we examine even the letter of James, which is supposed to concern itself much more with "good works" than with "faith," we find on examination that the letter is merely a corrective against false ideas of what "faith" implies. "Of what use is it," says James in effect, "if you do see the unseen realities of God, His Kingdom, and His Order, unless that perception is expressed and worked out in ordinary human situations?" That is a very proper question, and it is part of the discipline of life that, although we may have our glimpses of the glory of God, though we may by faith thoroughly accept the truth of the "Incarnation," the "Atonement," the "Resurrection," and so on, all these shining revolutionary truths have to be expressed and worked out in the dust and darkness, even in the strain and squalor of the sinful human situation. Far from decrying the value of faith, James is concerned to prevent such a faculty from becoming romantically airborne. He is determined, and rightly determined, that just as the young Prince of Glory lived His matchless life in the dust and sweat of the human arena, so users of the faith faculty must not consider themselves above their Lord.

It is, of course, when we come to the Letters of Paul that we find the word "faith" used again and again. It is used in slightly different senses, as we shall see in a moment, but always it includes this idea of grasping a reality, a whole dimension of reality which we cannot see with our fleshly senses. Paul indeed draws the strong contrast between the man whose vision and outlook is limited to this world and the man who, by the action of the Spirit, becomes alive to spiritual realities.

One of Paul's most important teachings, though it is only one, is the doctrine of what we call "justification by faith." It frequently appears to the non-Christian mind that this is an immoral or at least unmoral doctrine. Paul appears to be saying that a man is justified before God not by his goodness or badness, not by his good deeds or bad deeds, but by believing in a certain doctrine of the Atonement.

Of course, when we come to examine the matter more closely we can see that there is nothing unmoral in this teaching at all. For if "faith" means using a God-given faculty to apprehend the unseen divine order, and means, moreover, involving oneself in that order by personal commitment, we can at once see how different that is from merely accepting a certain view of Christian redemption. What Paul is concerned to point out again and again is that no man can reconcile himself to the moral perfection of God by his own efforts in this time-and-space setup. It is a foregone conclusion that he must fail. The truth is—and of course it is a truth which can only be seen and accepted by the faith faculty—that God has taken the initiative, that, staggering as it may seem, one of the main objects of the Personal Visit was to reconcile man to Himself. That which man in every religion, every century, every country, was powerless to effect, God has achieved by the devastating humility of His action and suffering in Jesus Christ. Now, accepting such an action as a *fait accompli* is only possible by this perceptive faculty of "faith." It requires not merely intellectual assent but a shifting of personal trust from the achievements of the self to the completely undeserved action of God. To accept this teaching by mind and heart does indeed require a *metanoia*, a revolution in the outlook of both mind and heart. Although the natural human personality sometimes regards this generous fact of reconciliation as an affront to its pride, to countless people since Paul's day it has been, as it was meant to be, Good News.

The phrase "justification by faith," then, simply means acceptance of a forgiveness and a reconciliation made by God Himself, and the total abandonment of efforts at self-justification. God's action, His "grace," as Paul calls it, becomes effectual when the truth of the matter becomes real by "faith." That is why Paul repeats again and again in different words his great theme, "By grace are ye saved through faith; and that not of yourselves: it is the gift of God." [13]

It appears to me that no little part of the joy and certainty of the early Christians springs from their wholehearted acceptance of this grace. In my own experience, limited as it may be, the glorious certainty of the early Church has been replaced today by a kind of wavering hopefulness, by no means free from attempts at self-justification. If we are to recapture the buoyancy and vigor

[13] Ephesians 2:8.

of New Testament Christians, we must stop quibbling about the question of our own forgiveness and our own standing with God. We must accept the generosity of God and stand upright as His sons and daughters. The attitude of the New Testament Letters in general is never one of dwelling upon man's sinfulness (even though it was sometimes necessary to remind people of what they *were*), but an encouraging looking forward to what they might become through the grace and power of God.

It is to Paul chiefly that we owe the thought (which is also found in John's letter) that Christ Himself lives in men's hearts. No one could read with an open mind the Letters of the New Testament without seeing that people are being, sometimes suddenly and sometimes step by step, transformed. The reason for this, according to Paul, is an open secret. In the past, he says in effect, men have striven to please an external God; now God's great secret is plain. With the coming of the Good News—indeed it is part of the Good News—God is prepared to live within the personalities of those who use their faculty of faith toward Him.[14] In Paul's writings we do not read of Jesus Christ as an Example Who lived and died some years before and Who must be followed and imitated. On the contrary, Paul's letters are ablaze with the idea that, if men will believe it, Christ is alive and powerful, ready to enter and transform the lives of even the most unlikely. This happens, he says, "by faith." But how rarely in present-day Christianity do we meet such a faith! Many Christians do not appear to have grasped this, one of the essentials of the Gospel. It is true that they believe in God; they pray to God and they try to follow the example of Christ. But, as far as one can tell, they have not begun to realize that Christ could be living and active at the very

[14] Colossians 1:26–27.

center of their own personalities. And of course so long as they do not believe it, it is not true for them. For just as in the days of Christ's human life the divine power was inhibited or limited by the absence of faith, so His activity within the personality is limited where a man does not in his heart of hearts believe in it. If we modern Christians are steadfastly refusing to believe in this inward miracle, it is not surprising that our Christian life becomes a dreary drudge.

In general, then, in Paul's writings faith means the grasping of the new, assured position in relation to God, the bold exploration of God's resources by use of the faith faculty, and the firm belief that Christ Himself is present and potent in the heart and soul of the Christian. At the same time, the same faith enables the Christian to see through this world's values, to be successful in refusing to be impressed by circumstances, good or bad, and to realize who he really is—a son of God whose permanent home is not here but in God's real home. "I reckon," says Paul, "that whatever we may have to go through now is less than nothing compared with the glorious future that God has prepared for us." [15] These words have no flavor of boastfulness, but ring perfectly true. If we feel that our own convictions fall a very long way short of such certainty, as I think we are bound to feel, can we not rightly conclude that people like Paul had developed the faculty of faith until it had the solidity of conviction, while for many of us it would be true to say that our faith has got little beyond a certain hopeful trustfulness?

It is obvious that if there are spiritual enemies of the sons and daughters of God (and who, if he has ever tried to live the life of a Christian, would deny it?), then the basic assault will be made upon the faculty of faith. If

[15] Romans 8:18.

only we can be maneuvered into the position of distrusting or disusing our faith faculty, then the battle is over; we are defeated men. It is not surprising to read of Paul's urging his convert Timothy to "fight the good fight of faith," [16] nor of Peter in his first letter speaking of the tensions and strains to which faith will be subjected once we see its enormous value. Appearances, feelings, even sometimes common sense, will undermine, if they can, the Christian's hold on ultimate reality, that is, his faith. It is not always easy to believe. If the good purpose of God were readily discernible there would have been no need for Jesus, for example, to urge men to have faith in God, nor for His apostles to do all they could to strengthen and confirm men's faith. There are failures as well as successes recorded in the New Testament, and Demas was surely neither the first nor the last to find the effort to live the life of faith too strenuous for his tastes.

"Faith" in Today's World

If we are genuinely willing to welcome the fresh wind of the Spirit and to experience once again the God-given vigor of the early Church, we must plainly begin by reusing the faculty of faith. Perhaps it would be not out of place here to make a few suggestions which for convenience' sake may be numbered:

1. Let us deliberately take time to consider our modern situation, not so much its problems but its attitude of mind and spirit. A few chapters read from the Acts of the Apostles might help us to appreciate by contrast how closed we have grown on the God-ward side. Perhaps we might, with as fresh minds as we can, read some of the Gospel incidents as well so that we may become convinced afresh that the fault in our present-day Christianity

[16] 1 Timothy 6:12.

lies not in God with His astonishing generosity, but in our own neglected capacity to believe, to reach out and appropriate His resources. Although we are not responsible for our talents or lack of them, we are very largely responsible for our own attitude of mind. Let us without morbid self-accusing confess that we have largely neglected to use our God-given faculty of faith. Let us freely admit that at heart our life attitude has been a long way from that of men attuned to unseen realities.

2. Let us by conscious and deliberate effort begin to exercise the long-disused faculty. Whatever our circumstances may be, life is so arranged that there is never a lack of opportunity for such exercise. It is apparent that, both for considering our own position in relation to God and for deliberately using our power of faith, we need a quiet space in our lives. This is absolutely essential, and nothing is more important than securing this space amid all our busy-ness. No one is too busy to set aside a period of, say, a quarter of an hour each day for such quiet. (We are all rather ridiculous here. For if we knew for certain that a space of a quarter of an hour's quiet was essential for our physical health, for example, we should unhesitatingly make room for it. It would become a top priority. Can we not see that such a period, which should be regarded as a minimum, could be absolutely essential for our spiritual health?) For many people this period of quiet must of necessity be solitary; but since a great deal of the vigor of the early Church depended on Christian fellowship and was in fact given and demonstrated through Christian fellowship, there is good reason to suppose that a small God-seeking group of people might help one another enormously in redeveloping the faith faculty.

3. Study of the New Testament with as unbiased and

unprejudiced a mind as possible will undoubtedly stimulate faith itself and the desire to develop the faculty more. Before long we cannot help realizing, if we "soak" ourselves in the meaning and spirit of these inspired pages, that this other world, which we have been in the habit of regarding as shadowy and far away, can, and in fact historically did, permeate ordinary human life. Further, we shall conclude that there is no valid reason for supposing that if the right conditions are fulfilled the same suprahuman quality and power could not penetrate life today.

4. Jesus told men "to knock," "to seek," and "to ask," by which I understand Him to mean that although the resources of God are always available, it is up to us men to make use of them. I think, too, that He may well have meant men to make spiritual experiments, to try out, as it were, the Divine resource. As we do this, we shall inevitably find that the values and fortunes of this passing world become less important and clamant. Nevertheless, I think we should be wise, by deliberately training ourselves, to see that real security does not, indeed cannot, rest in this world, however lucky or careful we may be. Moreover, all experiences of love and beauty, much as we may enjoy and appreciate them in this transitory life, are not rooted here at all. We should save ourselves a lot of disillusionment and heartbreak if we reminded ourselves constantly that here we have "no continuing city." [17] The world is rich with all kinds of wonders and beauties, but we only doom ourselves to disappointment if we think that the stuff of this world is permanent: its change and decay are inevitable. The rich variety of transitory beauty is no more than a reflection or a foretaste of the real and the permanent. Something surely of this thought is included in

[17] Hebrews 13:14.

Christ's words, "Lay up for yourselves treasures in Heaven, where neither moth nor rust doth corrupt, and where thieves do not break through nor steal." [18]

5. Finally, we must accept as one of the facts of life that to live on this level and to retain this attitude of mind and heart are not as easy as falling off a log. Sometimes, it is true, to do so is easy and natural, but there are other times when contemporary pressures and even our own lethargy make it difficult to rise and live as sons and daughters of the Most High. We must cheerfully accept the fact that, cost what it may, for the time being "we walk by faith, not by sight." [19] To exercise faith will often mean an effort on our part, a determined breaking through of the matted layers of this world's self-sufficiency, and a persistent reaching out to touch the living God.

[18] Matthew 6:20.   [19] 2 Corinthians 5:7.

Ground for Hope

The second great quality which New Testament Christianity exhibits seems to me to be Hope. Hope runs high in the inspired pages; it is not a superior form of pious wishful thinking but hope based solidly upon the character and purpose of God Himself. But for us, during the last fifty years particularly, the quality of hope has ebbed away from our common life almost imperceptibly. I say again that we are affected far more than we know, far more than we should be, by the prevailing atmosphere of thought around us. Christians, at any rate as far as western Europe is concerned, do not seem to exhibit much more hope than their non-Christian contemporaries. There is an unacknowledged and unexpressed fear in the hearts of many people that somehow the world has slipped beyond the control of God. Their reason may tell them that this cannot be so, but the constant assault of world tensions and the ever present threat of annihilation by nuclear weapons make people feel that the present setup is so radically different that the old rules no longer apply. Without realizing it, many of us are beginning to consent in our inmost hearts to the conclusion that we live in a hopeless situation.

It is very interesting to look back to the bouncing optimism of a period only fifty or sixty years ago. I have in my possession bound volumes of two of England's most popular magazines for the years 1897 to 1903. As may be imagined, they make fascinating reading. Britain's star is in the ascendant and she is unquestionably the richest and most powerful country in the world. Both the cost of living and the level of taxation are fantastically low. Most industries appear to be booming. The genie of Science is just beginning to be put to the service of mankind, and its boundless possibilities fill the scene with hope. Already aeroplanes and airships are forecast; the radio-telephone and even broadcasting and television are prophesied as being just around the corner. The total conquest of disease is looked forward to as something not very far ahead in man's triumphant forward progress. In the glossy pages of these magazines you get the general impression that the dark ages are safely behind and that man will now stride confidently forward in the light of Science. It is not without significance that among the contributors to these magazines there frequently appears the name of that gifted scientific humanist Mr. H. G. Wells.

This safe, comfortable world with its boundless optimism was shattered for ever by the 1914–1918 War. I do not think that ever again has that hopeful, almost bumptiously hopeful, atmosphere reappeared in this country. Quickly or slowly people began to see that science by itself is not enough, and that trust in human nature by itself is not enough. Mr. H. G. Wells himself died in bitter disillusionment, having just completed a book written out of his frantic disappointment and called *Mind at the End of Its Tether.*

The Second World War put a final end to any easy hopes or shallow optimism, and, except in places which are particularly fortunate or where people do not think or read about what is happening to the world, we do not find today any trace of those shining hopes of the early 1900's. Indeed, that particular kind of hope, so well expressed and illustrated in these old magazines, seems almost incredible to us today. It is not simply that we have become disillusioned about human nature through the evidence of two world wars and the contemporary evidence of atheistic Communism today, but that all of us are far more aware of the world with its tensions and problems than our cheerful forefathers could ever have been. Vastly improved methods of communication and travel have meant the end of a safe, complacent "parochial" outlook. Even if we try to detach ourselves personally from the world's burdens, we are assailed by newspapers, radio, and television, and we can scarcely help feeling something of the world's pains and problems. This I venture to think is by no means altogether a bad thing, for it means that for the very first time in human history a great many intelligent men and women are realizing how interdependent we are as human beings. Nations, even whole continents, are awakening from the sleep of centuries, and while violent nationalism flares up from time to time, there is a growing sense among responsible people of all nations that we are "all in it together." If we are to have hope amidst all the menaces and threats of today's world, it has got to be a sturdy and well founded hope. There can never be a return to the shallow optimism of those whose outlook was both narrow and complacent.

At this point we must distinguish between what is genuine hope and what was called in the Second World War "wishful thinking." Hope must always be based upon realities, in the end upon God, the great Reality. But wishful thinking, though it often sounds like hope, is nothing more than an expression of what we should like to happen. Of course, in our ordinary speech we all of us say such things as, "I hope so-and-so," when all we really mean is that we *wish* so-and-so would happen. This does not matter very much in common parlance as long as we are quite clear in our own minds that there is a definite distinction between expressing a wish and possessing a hope with real grounds for it. For example, a young man may say, "I hope I have got through this exam." If he has worked hard and done a good paper, the hope is perfectly genuine. But if in fact he has done little or no work beforehand, and answered the paper carelessly, it is not a genuine hope; it is merely an expression of his wishes. Now, being human, we all do this kind of thing from time to time. A man may quite naturally say, "I hope I don't die of some painful disease," or, "I hope I don't live to be a burden to my relations." This is perfectly understandable and right, but not a hope—only an expression of what he *wishes* may happen.

We could, then, fairly say without being at all cynical that a very great deal of what passes for hope today is either wishful expectation or the expressed reaction of a mind which is not prepared to face realities. We shall not find in the New Testament, I think, a single instance of hope used in any but its genuine sense, that is, hope rooted in the good Purpose of God. You will remember how James in his New Testament letter is particularly severe in his condemnation of the "pious hope" for other people's good which does nothing practical to implement the wish.[1] He says in effect that if you should see people cold or hungry or without proper clothes, and you say, "Well, God bless you—I hope you will soon be all right!" what on earth is the good of that? This sort of pious hope is still with us. People will say, for example, "I do hope they will soon find a cure for cancer," but many of them would not

[1] James 2:15-16.

dream of giving a penny to any anticancer research fund. Or they will say, "I do hope something is done for all those thousands and thousands of poor refugees and homeless people over there in Europe." But not one in a hundred who expresses such a hope does anything to make it come true. We have to rid our minds of both pious hopes and wishful thinking before we get down to solid, genuine hope.

The inspired writings of the New Testament are neither optimistic nor pessimistic; they are very far from being the enthusiastic outpourings of people expressing their ideals and painting rosy pictures of a dream world which might one day be true. Nor, on the other hand, do the writers underline the sinfulness and depravity of human nature. We are reading what was written by men at first-hand grips with realities, and it is both astonishing and heartening to find how hopeful they are. Unless we happen to have studied ancient history, we may not have realized how remarkable are the bright hopes of the early band of Christians. The surrounding pagan world was dark; it was full of fear, cruelty, and superstition. For the most part the old religions had failed. Human life had become cheap; common morality was in many cases very lightly regarded; and belief in a world to come was almost nonexistent. The English poet Swinburne, probably feeling that Victorian piety had taken away the joy and color from life, wrote these bitter words about Christ:

"Thou hast conquered, O pale Galilean; the world has grown grey from Thy breath."

But if Swinburne had studied the history of the Church immediately following the death of the "pale Galilean," he would have found that exactly the reverse was true. The surrounding world was indeed gray, sometimes black with corruption and all kinds of evil, but in the Young Church there was gay and indomitable hope. Nothing could quench this hope, for these men and women now knew through Christ what God was like, and they now knew for certain that death was a defeated enemy. While the pagan world had largely become sodden with self-indulgence and ridden by the fear of death, the brave new fellowship of believers in Christ was a light and a flame in the darkness; it was a fellowship of hope.

All hope in the New Testament, as I have said above, rests upon the Nature and Purpose of God. These men and women are hopeful because, as Jesus Christ told men, "with God all things are possible." [2] Those who had come to believe with complete conviction that God loves the world, that He has visited it in Person and shown His power in transforming the lives of the most unlikely characters, were not readily disposed to lose hope in His ultimate Purpose. But of course that hope was not limited to the present temporary scene that we call life. The center of gravity of their hope was in the eternal and not in the temporal world. This was the quality which both baffled and infuriated their enemies as fierce persecution began to arise. The pagan world with its ever present horror of death could scarcely believe the evidence of their senses when they found in the Christian martyrs men and women to whom death was not a disaster at all. To the pagan mind to take a man's life was to take his all, but to attack Christians by sword, torture, or the atrocities of the arena was to invite defeat. Even if you killed them they slipped through your fingers to be with their Lord for ever!

Although New Testament Christians doubtless prayed, as we do, "Thy Kingdom come, Thy Will be done on Earth, as it is in Heaven," and although they therefore

[2] Mark 10:27.

doubtless worked and prayed for the improvement of the world in which they lived, their hope rested upon God, not merely upon what He could do in this world, but upon His high, mysterious Purpose. Of comparatively recent years the center of our faith has become, at any rate in some quarters, more and more earthbound. We are concerned with the Christian attitude to housing, to social problems, to juvenile delinquency, to international relationships, and indeed to every department of human life. This is fine as far as it goes, but sometimes one gets the impression that Christians are "falling over backwards" to disavow their otherworldliness. Yet to have the soul firmly anchored in Heaven rather than grounded in this little sphere is far more like New Testament Christianity.

In the here-and-now there are many flagrant injustices which remain unjudged, many problems which remain unsolved, and many loose ends which are never tied up. There are also, in the transitory life of this planet, serious limitations which God has imposed upon His own working through the risky gift of what we call "free will." Such factors as sheer ignorance, lack of faith, disobedience, or downright refusal to obey the truth quite plainly inhibit the operation of the Spirit of God. We can read how such things inhibited the power of Jesus Christ Himself and similarly limited the power of the vigorous Young Church. If Christian hope were a kind of optimistic humanism restricted merely to what happens in this passing world it would be a poor lookout indeed. As Paul pointedly remarked, "If in this life only we have hope in Christ, we are of all men most miserable." [3]

Yet, as we look at today's Christians, is it not true that many of them are earthbound? They have been affected far more than they know by the Communist gibe about

[3] 1 Corinthians 15:19.

"pie in the sky" and similar thrusts suggesting that Christianity deals with the shadowy "spiritual" values, and refers all insoluble "real" difficulties to an imaginary Heaven. The suggestion is that the politician, the psychiatrist, the social worker, the doctor, the nurse, and a host of others are left to cope with the tensions and muddles of the here-and-now. Christians have sometimes allowed themselves to be swayed more than they should be by jeers at their "spiritual" and "otherworldly" point of view. In defense they make a determined effort to prove that the Christian Faith is extremely relevant in every department of human existence. Consequently it is not uncommon, at any rate in this country, to have a positive riot of advertising the Faith under such titles as "Christianity and the Home," "Christianity and the Family," "Christianity and World Peace," "Christianity and Daily Work," "Christianity and Local Government," "Christianity and Education," "Christianity and Sex," and so on. Now all this is fine as far as it goes, for it is undeniably true that when people owe a heart loyalty to Jesus Christ it will affect the way they behave in all their human relationships. But Christianity is not a kind of salve which can be applied to a given human situation. It is and has always been a matter of winning individuals to give their heart loyalty to Christ and to the fellowship of Christians. From such a fellowship Christians can indeed permeate the society in which they live and work. But to say, for example, "If only all schoolteachers were practicing Christians how wonderful the world would be!" is a waste of time. You cannot apply Christianity "in the mass" like that. Even in the most vigorous and flourishing days of the Young Church the followers of the Way were a tiny minority. It can do no harm to point out from time to time how revolutionized our various institutions would be if their members were all practicing Christians. But if this is the limit of our hope, we are laying up for ourselves bitter disappointment.

The Christian who is spiritually linked to the timeless life of God, and who is, not by courtesy title but in reality, a son of God, cannot escape a certain painful tension throughout his earthly life. He is only a temporary resident here; his home, his treasure, the final fulfillment of his hope do not lie in this transitory life at all. He must resist the temptation to withdraw from this benighted, sin-infected world and spend all his spare time in pietistic reflection of the world to which he is bound. He must hold fast to the belief that God is active and contemporary, working wherever He is given opportunity, in the present passing scene. "My Father is busy up to this very moment," said Christ, "and so am I." [4] The servant is in the same position as his Master. He too must be busy as his Father is busy. His love and concern must be to some degree a reflection of the God Who "so loved the world" that He would go to any length to rescue and redeem it. But if the world rejects the truth, if the world willfully refuses to follow the revealed pattern of living, the Christian need not for one moment think that the Faith to which he is committed has failed, even if to the very end of what we call time upon this planet those who own allegiance to the Unseen King remain a small minority. This does not disprove the truth and validity of the Christian Faith. Seen, so to speak, from the angels' point of view, it is simply the tragedy of one little planet refusing to see and recognize the Light. After what we call death the Christian will be able to see the significance of the next stage. It would indeed be difficult to find any evidence in the New Testament that the end of this earthly experiment that we call life is the world-wide acceptance of Christ and

[4] John 5:17.

the universal establishment of His Kingdom. Many excellent Christians seem to regard this as the ultimate goal of Christian teaching, preaching, worshiping, and witnessing. Yet as far as I can discover, apart from cheery hymns usually sung in optimistic periods between world wars, this rosy view belongs entirely to isolated texts of Scripture. One is, "For the earth shall be filled with the knowledge of the glory of the Lord, as the waters cover the sea." [5] I for one am rather doubtful whether that is meant to be a prophecy of the universal acceptance of Christ. Another comes from that strange book in which John is told in one of his visions that "The kingdoms of this world are become the kingdoms of our Lord, and of His Christ; and He shall reign for ever and ever." [6] But this prophecy, if studied in its context, is a prophecy not of universal acceptance but of universal judgment. Truth has finally judged error, and that this is no popular event is shown in verse 18 when we read that "the nations were angry."

It is impossible without being dishonest to dismiss the question of New Testament hope without mentioning the Second Coming of Christ. We may freely admit that the early Christians were wrong in thinking that Christ would return in power within their lifetime. It is possible to detect in the writings of Paul, for example, a change of atmosphere in his letters to the Thessalonians (which were probably his earliest), and what is probably his last letter, the letter to Titus. But even in the latter Paul refers to the "looking for that blessed hope, and the glorious appearing of the great God and our Saviour Jesus Christ." [7] The hope may have become deferred in its fulfillment, but it is still a very real hope. New Testament Christians may well have modified their early views as to the imme-

[5] Habakkuk 2:14.   [6] Revelation 11:15.   [7] Titus 2:13.

diacy of Christ's return, yet the fact of His coming again in judgment of the world is always implicit in their thinking and hoping. We need to remember that among the early Christians were quite a number who were actually present when the Son of God ascended back to Heaven—a symbolic action, of course, but historically true. Such men would not readily forget the words of the heavenly messenger who told them quite plainly that "this same Jesus, which is taken up from you into heaven, shall so come in like manner as ye have seen him go into heaven." [8]

Unhappily for us, the whole subject of the Second Coming of Christ has been for many years the playground of cranks and fanatics. This has made us not only shy of dealing with the question ourselves but reluctant to believe in "the blessed hope" as a fact at all. Various people, especially within the last sixty years or so, have manipulated texts of Holy Scripture with little regard to context to prove that Christ would return on this or that day. For example, in my own experience I remember a man in 1934 hiring the Queen's Hall in London solemnly to warn the British Empire that Jesus Christ would return in Person on, I think, the 24th of June of that year. So convinced was he of his calculations that he stated at the time that if he were wrong he would "sink into well-merited obscurity." He left himself no loophole for later revision of the timetable as others have done, and I presume he still lives in his obscurity. This example is only one of hundreds of misguided people who have thought they could calculate what, on Jesus' own admission, was known only to the Father.[9] But I really don't see why, because this important New Testament hope has been the stamping ground of the fanatical, we should be cheated altogether

[8] Acts 1:11.   [9] Mark 13:32.

of what was essentially a part of early Christian teaching. Perhaps, as in other aspects of Christian truth, we need to look at the matter with fresh eyes.

With all the advancement of human knowledge in a score of different realms, we still have no clue at all as to the "why" of our existence on this planet. We may believe that the planet itself cooled down from a mass of gaseous vapor thrown off by the sun and that in several million years, in an ascending scale of living creatures, a self-conscious animal whom we call Homo sapiens finally appeared. Alternatively, we may believe that creation took place in a series of "leaps" and that the last leap forward corresponds to the time when primitive man emerged from the animal creation. Whichever view we hold, we are not given in the Bible, nor have we discovered elsewhere, very much in the way of explanation for the huge æon-long experiment that is being conducted on the surface of this planet. Christians believe, as has already been said, that this observable, detectable life is only the physical outcrop of a spiritual drama; that, although much of the life that we see around us in nature, in animals and in men, is physical or at least detectable by physical means, yet ultimately the significance of the whole affair is spiritual. The world is a temporary stage for man's actions, his body the temporary clothes for his life here only; the real meaning of things does not lie in their appearance but in what they signify. That, in passing, may explain why Christians are so disturbed with what they call the materialism of the present age. They are disturbed because the materialist cannot see beyond the material world. He thinks, in his blindness, that those things we at best use and enjoy in passing are somehow realities and to be pursued and enjoyed for their own sake. But the Christian accepts life as a preparation or training for something infinitely fuller and more satisfying that lies beyond the present physical limitations of existence. The Christian knows that this assumption is more than an assumption, for the moment he is aligned with the purpose and life of God through Christ he feels in his bones, if that is not too crude and earthly an expression, that he is now one with the timeless life of the universe. He refuses to give his heart to or be taken in by the values and pleasures of this passing world. He does not hesitate to use all that is good and beautiful and true, partly because he knows that his God gives him "richly all things to enjoy," [10] and partly because he knows that in all life's impermanent beauties and pleasures there is the promise of the real and permanent which he is thoroughly convinced will exceed his wildest expectations. But even the Christian, for all this satisfying and hopeful conviction, does not know the meaning of the mystery of life, and if he is wise he does not pretend to. He has enough light to light him on his way, but there are a great many gaps in his knowledge. When he says, "One day we shall understand," he is by no means always uttering a pious platitude. Quite frequently he is voicing a solid conviction, a genuine facet of hope. At present his vision is severely limited, and that is probably just as well if his sanity is to be preserved. But when he is free from the limitations of temporal life, he has every hope of being able to know as surely as he is at present known.[11]

To the Christian by far the most significant fact of history is the personal visit of God to this planet in the Person of Jesus Christ. He may well stand amazed at the manner of this quiet slipping into the stream of history. That humble birth in an obscure country is probably very far from the manner most of us would have chosen for the personal entry of the Son of God. The Christian simply

[10] 1 Timothy 6:17.   [11] 1 Corinthians 13:12.

does not know why empires rose and fell, why millions of ordinary people lived and loved and died in dozens of different nations before ever God decided the right moment had come for His personal visit to this planet. There must be a higher wisdom at work than mere human planning. Strip all the decoration away from the Christmas story, and we can see the almost incredible humility of that great act of God. Now, if the claims of Christ were true and we accept them, we do not argue about God's wisdom in choosing a particular family in a particular country at a particular time for the birth of Jesus because we know so little of the total issues involved; we simply accept an action of wisdom far higher than our own. To the neat and tidy mind of the human planner few things could be more untidy historically than the entry of God into the world nearly two thousand years ago. The might of Babylon, the wisdom of Egypt, and the glory of Greece had disappeared. The vast Roman Empire was already beginning to show signs of decay. Even the small nation of the Jews among whom God chose to be born had traveled a long way from its spiritual heyday. Some centuries had elapsed since there had been a genuine prophetic voice speaking the Word of the Lord, and the Holy Land was no more than an occupied territory of no great importance. The situation and conditions generally would hardly have seemed to any human planner opportune for so unique an occasion as the entry of God Himself into the world. Speaking reverently, if the planning had been in our hands we should probably have chosen that the Son of God should be born into one of the best families. We should like to have been sure that, from the point of view of education, culture, social contacts, and all those other things which we think are so important for our children, everything was ideally arranged for the most important Baby the world had ever seen. But how different is what God actually did from what we might have expected Him to do! The Divine Planning obviously springs from a knowledge and wisdom both higher and deeper than our own.

Planners as we are, if we envisage the Second Coming of Christ at all, we see Him returning in triumph upon a scene already largely perfected. We think it would be a fine thing if the world were neat and tidy, all problems were solved, all tensions were relaxed, understanding and friendship were world-wide, health and wealth were at their highest peak, when Christ returned, not this time as a helpless babe, but as a King in power and glory. Of one thing we can be quite certain: this high, unfathomable wisdom of God works on quite a different plane from any human planning. The time of the irruption of eternity into time, the moment for God to call the end to the long experiment that we call life, will not be made in consultation with human planners! Judging from His previous action in human history, God is perfectly capable of choosing an unusual and unlikely moment, as it will appear to human beings. Indeed, if we are to take the words of Jesus seriously, His return to the world or the winding up of the time and space setup, whichever way we look at it, is to be in the middle of strife, tension, and fear. In the letters of the New Testament it is the same: the coming of Christ is a blessed hope of intervention, not a personal appearance at a Utopian celebration.

Now if our hopes, whatever we protest, really lie in this world instead of in the eternal Order, we shall find it difficult to accept the New Testament teaching of the Second Coming. In our eyes the job is not yet done, and such an action would be, though we would not put it so, an interference. But suppose our hope rests in the purpose of God; then we safely leave the timing of the earthly experiment to Him. Meanwhile, we do what we were told to do—to be alert and to work and to pray for the spread of His Kingdom.

In the meantime it is essential that we recapture and hold fast the New Testament idea that God is the "God of hope." [12] In the New Testament writings there is a continual sense not only of the immediacy but of the contemporaneousness of God. Their authors can write realistically of the God of hope because they are very close in point of time to God's act of intervention in what nowadays we call the Incarnation, and because the power of the Young Church is very plainly and demonstrably the power of the living Spirit. Many modern Christians are inclined to put God back into the past. How many times in visiting various churches does one hear of what used to happen in the old days! And, since Christians derive a great deal of their inspiration from reading the Bible, they can all too easily envisage God as thoroughly at home in the sacred pages but somehow no part of the modern picture at all. In a former book [13] I recalled how I tested a group of young people by asking them to give a quick answer to the question "Do you think God understands radar?" And how the answer was "No," to be followed of course by laughter as the absurdity became apparent. But I am still convinced that the unpremeditated answer was highly significant and revealing. Without admitting it in so many words, many Christians today cannot readily conceive of God operating in a world of television, washing machines, atomic fission, automation, psychiatry, electronic brains, glossy magazines, modern music, and jet propulsion. The complication and speed of present-day living make it extremely difficult for the mind to imagine the Biblical God interpenetrating such a system and operating

[12] Romans 15:13.   [13] *Your God Is Too Small.*

within its pressures. The very word "God" seems out of key and even bizarre in our modern context.

Two things are necessary if we are to rediscover the buoyant hope of the New Testament. The first obvious step is to make certain that our hope is really hope and not either wishful thinking or merely pious hope. It must be closely allied to our faith and must ultimately be rooted in what we know for certain of the Nature and Purpose of God Himself. We might do well to study afresh the kind of hopes which sustained and inspired the Young Church and compare them with our own. This will naturally bring us to our next step, which is to rediscover the contemporaneousness of God. This may require a drastic revolution in our thinking, for we may discover that we have been thinking of God as Someone we can escape to, rather than Someone Who is actually not only in ourselves but in the noisy hurly-burly of everyday life. This does not mean to deny that modern life is distracting, complex, and difficult, but it does mean realizing afresh that God is not in the slightest degree baffled or bewildered by what baffles and bewilders us. It is no good longing for the monastic quiet of a past age or for the simplicity of life of a pastoral generation. Our urgent need is to discover God, the God of hope, in the present strain, in the complex problem, actually at work in the given situation. For He is either a present help or He is not much help at all.

Love

In English-speaking countries, at least, we breathe such an atmosphere of diffused traditional Christianity that we are apt to take some of the major Christian revelations about God as though they were self-evident, which of course they are not. We assume that kindness is a better thing than intolerance and love a better thing than hatred. But these elementary assumptions are only true if the Nature of the Author of the whole bewildering universe is Himself kind, understanding, and loving. Most people, whether inside or outside the churches, attempt at least to believe that "God is Love." Many non-Christians have not the faintest idea that this is a purely Christian concept, and that before the coming of the Gospel no nation in the world had ever dared to conceive of God as active Personal Love. Of course, the Old Testament contains many passages which refer to the love of God, but it would be fair to say that on the whole they are conditional. Put very crudely, the burden of the Old Testament messages in general is: "If you are good and obey the Lord He will be kind and will prosper you. But if you are disobedient and arouse His wrath then He will most surely destroy you." We might profitably compare this prevailing Old Testament atmosphere with Jesus' parable of the Father and the Prodigal Son,[1] or with His specific statement, "He is kind unto the unthankful and to the evil." [2]

"God" in various religions might be thought of as benevolent toward the mortal creation, but the reason that the Gospel was Good News when it first burst upon the world was simply that men had realized that God is Love. The revelation of character provided by Christ Himself, the awe-full brunt of suffering which He was prepared to bear in order to redeem mankind, His triumph over man's last enemy, His ascension to timeless reality, taking Human Nature with Him as it were; His continual coming by the Spirit to transform and reinforce men's lives—all these, the unshakable conviction of the Young Church, showed one thing: that God is by nature Love and that He loves mankind. Men who accepted this foundation truth found an indefinable endorsement of it in their own hearts. They also found that their own "love-energy," which had previously been turned in upon themselves or was being given to the wrong things, now became an outflowing love embracing their fellow men for whom Christ died. Further, this love not only changed in direction but in quality. It was something more than natural love; it began to resemble divine Love. Indeed, it is hardly an exaggeration to say that Christianity gave the word "love" a new and deeper meaning. The new love was stimulated and developed by accepting the love of God as shown in Christ. "If God then so loved us we ought also to love the brethren," wrote John.[3] The new life of faith and hope is made possible, according to Paul, "because the love of God is shed abroad in our hearts." [4]

I am quite sure that a great deal of the joyful experience and invincible courage of the Young Church is due

[1] Luke 15:11-32.
[2] Luke 6:35.
[3] 1 John 4:11.
[4] Romans 5:5.

simply to the fact that the early Christians believed these words to be literally true. To them nothing could alter this basic fact, and no experience of life could separate them from God's unremitting love. I have become absolutely convinced that what we need to recover, perhaps more than anything else, is the conviction that God is not merely kindly disposed toward us, but that He *is* Love. Some theology will not allow us to enjoy this beautiful simplicity. It is far too good to be true, and the implication seems to be that if we were allowed to take John's words at their face value we should all misbehave ourselves very badly. Consequently, we are often told that God's love is not to be imagined in terms of human love, that it is higher, deeper, truer, and sterner. In fact, if we are not very much on our guard we are cheated of the Good News —the inestimable comfort of knowing that God is Love is whisked away and we are given instead something so poor, unbending, and relentless that instead of being reassured and inspired we are repulsed and frightened. The Divine Lover has become "the Hound of Heaven."

Now of course, like every other clergyman and minister, I am familiar with the arguments which surround the Love of God with any number of caveats and provisos. Those who arrogate to themselves the task of interpreting God's Love frequently cannot bear it to be either universal or vulnerable. Yet if there is one lesson above all which is borne out by the awe-full spectacle of the Crucifixion of the Son of God, it is that His Love *is* vulnerable. It is not a conditional love; it is an openhearted, generous self-giving which God offers to men. Those who would carefully limit the operation of God's Love to people who fulfill certain conditions, usually of their own making, have missed the point. Their Gospel is not "God is Love" but "God is love if you will fulfill the conditions which we will outline to you." The risk of proclaiming God's unconditional love toward mankind is precisely the same risk which God Himself took in becoming Man in Christ. People sometimes talk as though there would be a carelessness or even flippancy about living if John's words were taken at their face value. But is this really true? Is it not simply that those who are secretly afraid of God or who secretly hate Him are themselves lacking in love? And is it not equally true that those who have grasped something of the amazing love of God are most filled with generous love toward others?

I must say at this point that I am profoundly disturbed by the technique of several modern evangelists, though not, thank God, of all. This technique is to arouse feelings of guilt and fear, which is not too difficult in many sensitive, conscientious people, and, having got people thoroughly miserable about their sins, to point them to the Saviour. Of course, the Old Testament is dredged to provide ammunition for this kind of spiritual assault, and indeed it is not a very arduous task to find texts from the Old Testament prophets which, ripped from their context, can produce the guilt feeling which many modern evangelists so earnestly desire. If these men are right, then one is driven to the conclusion that both Jesus Himself and the Young Church were wrong in their methods. Jesus Himself called men by a positive and not a negative method. It was only the religious and the hypocritical who called forth His salvos of denunciation. As the Young Church moved forward into the world we read nothing of this method of guilt stimulation. (Of course, guilt was aroused both on the Day of Pentecost by Peter's speech and subsequently by the speech of Stephen before his martyrdom. This is plainly because the Jews were made to realize that they were corporately responsible for the murder of Jesus Who was in fact God's Christ. We do not find in the Acts of the Apostles a similar reaction when the Gospel is preached outside Jerusalem.) It was *Good* News which the Young Church proclaimed—that God was known, that death was conquered, that the essential reconciliation had been made and that man had only to place his central trust in the Man Christ Jesus to find that he was at one with God and could be filled through all his being with the Spirit of God. This is not to deny, of course, the reality of human sin or that it must be forgiven by God; but the technique of arousing fear and guilt, that is, the negative approach, is not the New Testament method. The declaration of the love of God and the shining possibility of men and women becoming His sons and daughters are the keynotes of the New Testament proclamation of the Gospel. We are all indoctrinated far more than we know, and it would do us a world of good if we would study the methods of Jesus Christ and the methods of the Young Church at first hand, without being influenced by the tendentious aid of "chain references" and "edited" handling of the New Testament which drive us to conclusions into which a fair-minded reading would never lead us.

If it is true that God is Love, then it follows that, as John so clearly points out, "every one that loveth is born of God, and knoweth God." [5] This we shall find absolutely true to life's experience and to our own. It is when we love, even a little, that we sense a kinship with the Nature of things. For instance, in the course of true love between a man and a woman, or in the experience of parents with their newborn child—that is, at times of special sensitivity—many ordinary people feel that they are somehow touching Reality. Similarly, those who devote their lives

[5] 1 John 4:7.

wholeheartedly to the service of, shall we say, deaf, blind, or mentally defective children not infrequently find a satisfying sense that they are in accord with some purpose much greater than themselves. Examples could be multiplied again and again, but in the experience of ordinary people, without any particular religious faith, the actions of real love sometimes announce themselves as part of the divine Love. The opposite is equally true. However religious a man may be, however correct his beliefs and punctilious his ritual observances, unless he loves he does not know God.

It is peculiarly salutary to reflect that in the earthly life of Jesus His bitterest enemies were the respectably religious, whose god was their own righteousness. By far the most determined persecution of the Young Church, as recorded in the Acts of the Apostles, came from those who were religiously orthodox but who had never learned to love.

Of course, the touching of reality accidentally, as it were, by the normal giving of the human heart, can remain no more than a passing feeling. Its significance, its tremendous significance, can easily be missed. That is why so many pages were spent above in writing of the faculty of faith. For unless a man is prepared to use his faculty of faith and grasp the fact that God is Love, he will never rise above the level of being an "unconscious Christian," to his own loss and the loss of the Christian fellowship which we call the Church. This country, at least, has many thousands of such unconscious Christians. These men and women need to be told that what they are following, often spasmodically, is indeed ultimate reality and has been focused for us all in the recorded life of Jesus Christ. They already know something of love, but the garbled version of the Gospel which they hear from certain high-pressure evangelists does nothing to associate in their minds the ideas of "love" and of "God." How early Paul saw the full truth we do not precisely know, but certainly in 1 Corinthians 13 he has reached a point of insight which is quite miraculous in a man with his training and background. He sees now with the utmost clarity that whatever tremendous and impressive things he may accomplish, however wide and deep his knowledge, however strong his faith, if he has no love he amounts to nothing at all.

Because all Christians (however hard-boiled they may be in the liquor of the special tenets of their own denominational party) realize to some extent the truth of Paul's words, we find them at least attempting to love. But all those who try to love are beset by certain temptations of which these are the chief:

1. *The temptation to imitate love.* It has truly been said that we only grow in character when we are "real," and if we merely force ourselves to act as loving Christians we do not learn to love, nor do we grow in love. Yet this sort of acting, even though it be unconscious, is quite common among Christians and probably plays some part in all of our lives. We need to do a little honest self-examination here and to realize that no spiritual progress is made and no lasting spiritual growth occurs without honesty. If we find we cannot love, it is of no use at all to cover up our failure by a pretense. It is far better to turn to God Who is Love and freely admit our deficiency and allow the Spirit of God to change our inner attitude and produce the genuine fruit of love.

I believe a good deal of nonsense is talked about the business of "liking" and "loving." I have listened to several sermons in which the congregation has been told in effect that we cannot help our likes and dislikes and that the most God expects of us toward those we dislike is to act as though we loved them. Of course, the first part of this contention is true; for reasons of which we are largely unconscious we may instinctively dislike, perhaps violently dislike, certain people even though they be with us in the Christian fellowship. That is a situation common to nearly all of us. But is the real solution to "act" as though we love such people? I believe there is a better and more constructive part for the Christian to pursue. Jesus told us to pray for those who despitefully use us and persecute us,[6] and if the greater includes the less I should imagine that includes those who "get on our nerves," "rub us up the wrong way," "get in our hair," or whatever expression we use privately about them. I make no pretense that this is an easy path to pursue, but I do suggest that if we pray for those who annoy and irritate us and whom we dislike, our dislike is lessened and our understanding is increased. We must naturally be perfectly honest about it. We must say to Him Who is the Father of us all, in all honesty and simplicity: "I hate the sight of So-and-So. He (or she) irritates me beyond endurance and always brings out the worst in me. Help me to pray for him (or her)." It takes considerable courage to embark on this course of action, but the situation is invariably improved, and sometimes it is revolutionized. In praying for a person's real self we grow immeasurably in tolerance and understanding, and it is not unknown for instinctive dislike to be transformed into respect, understanding, and even love. But this will never happen if we insist on maintaining an inner attitude of "I can't help it: I always have disliked So-and-So and I always will."

Now naturally, since any change of inward attitude normally takes time, we have got to "act" (and act in love)

[6] Matthew 5:44.

justly and fairly toward those whom we dislike, but purely as an interim way of behavior and not as our final attitude.

There is a further danger of imitation love. It is perfectly possible for us to behave kindly, justly, and correctly toward one another and yet withhold that giving of the "self" which is the essence of love. Married people will perhaps more easily appreciate what I am trying to say. A husband may behave with perfect kindness and consideration toward his wife; he may give her a generous allowance; he may do more than his share of the household chores, and indeed he may do all the things which an ideal husband is supposed to do. But if he withholds "himself" the marriage will be impoverished. Women who seem to know these things intuitively would infinitely prefer the husband to be less kind, considerate, and self-sacrificing if they were only sure that he with all his imperfections and maddening ways gave "himself" in love in the marriage. This principle applies to some extent to all human relationships, and I am quite certain that it is this costly, self-giving love which Paul had in mind in 1 Corinthians 13. Many, even among Christians, shrink from it, not I think because they are afraid to give but because they are afraid that their gift will not be appreciated; in short, that they may be hurt. But surely this is the risk that love must always take, and without this giving of the self with all the risks that that entails, love is a poor pale imitation. "Consider *him*," [7] writes the author of the Epistle to the Hebrews, and if we do we find this is precisely the sort of rejectable, vulnerable love Christ lived and died to prove.

2. *The temptation to hate oneself.* The cheerful pagan takes himself as a rule very much for granted, but

[7] Hebrews 12:3.

the Christian who is sooner or later brought face to face with Truth is disgusted and dispirited to find how self-loving and self-centered his life really is. The more he comes into contact with the living Christ, the more he realizes there is to be put right, and if he is not careful his normal pride and self-respect go suddenly "into reverse." The more he thinks of the standards of love and those who live by them, the more wrong he feels, until he ends with a thoroughgoing contempt for himself and all his doings. The self with whom he has lived for some years in reasonable comfort becomes an intolerable person; before long he has slipped into despising himself wholeheartedly. Now this, despite what some religious books have said, is a thoroughly bad state of mind in which to live. The man who despises or hates himself will sooner or later, despite all his religious protestations, reveal hatred and contempt for his brother men. Whatever his profession of love for "sinners," the contempt for the sin which he has found in himself is all too easily projected onto those who sin.

At this point we need to consider the sane words of Jesus Christ Himself. According to Him, the second great commandment for a man is to "love thy neighbor as thyself." [8] These words, I am sure, contain no accidental lapse of speech. We do naturally love ourselves, and no spiritual contortions or inverted pride can ever alter the fact. Surely what Jesus is urging is that that love, that understanding, that "making allowance" which we normally use for ourselves should be extended and used to embrace others. It is true that in other places Jesus says that a man should "deny himself," [9] but this surely carries the force of denying his own egotistical temptations. It means self-

[8] Matthew 22:39; Mark 12:31.
[9] Matthew 16:24; Mark 8:34; Luke 9:23.

forgetfulness instead of self-interest; it means voluntary self-giving but not self-contempt.

This business of hating oneself, though it appears virtuous, is in reality one of Satan's most plausible devices. It keeps a man preoccupied with himself and his sins; it puts part of a man in a very superior position from which he can look down and despise the rest of himself. We might well reflect something like this, "If God loves me for all my faults and peculiarities, who am I to say that I am not worth loving?" The abject attitude of self-loathing may be natural in the presence of God's holiness, but never do we find in the Bible that God requires its continuance. Having seen and admitted our faults, the command is to stand, or go, or do. We are all of us very far from perfect, but God does not wait for our perfection before He can use us in His purposes, a fact for which we can be grateful, and the business of transforming us from within always takes time. Let us, without being complacent or self-indulgent, come to good-humored terms with ourselves. It is a good thing to see how far we are off course, but no good purpose is served by despising ourselves for having been such poor pilots. It is a strange thing how hard it is for most of us to laugh at ourselves. We would far rather despise ourselves as sinners, even the chief of sinners, than laugh at ourselves as self-important little idiots! The plank in our own eye[10] probably provokes the angels to a good deal of laughter, but in our precious dignity we would rather have orgies of contrition and repentance and self-loathing than the healthy gust of one good-humored laugh at ourselves.

3. *The temptation to separate love of God from love of people.* "The more I see of some people, the more

[10] Matthew 7:3; Luke 6:41.

I love my dog," runs the modern half-humorous comment. Of course, it is far easier to love a devoted animal who more than rewards us by the utmost fidelity and affection than it is to love people who in addition to being much more complex beings often do not reward us at all. Similarly, it is easy to love humanity without loving people. Many of the greatest crimes against individual living people have been committed in the name of love for humanity. There are plenty of people with us today who will talk about world peace and the universal brotherhood of man but who cannot get on with their own families or neighbors. People, in fact, unless they happen to be our own special friends, are quite difficult to love.

Naturally, Jesus knew this very well and he connected inseparably the love of God with the love of other people. Indeed, it is part of the act of incarnation that God and human beings are indissolubly wedded. This is the kind of fact which most of us would rather not have to face. It is comparatively easy for us to imagine God as the Perfection of all beauty, truth, and love and to respond with worship and adoration to such a Being. What we find almost too much to stomach is that this very same God has allied Himself through Christ with ordinary human beings. In Jesus' famous parable of the Last Judgment,[11] men find to their astonishment that their treatment of fellow human beings is adjudged to be the same thing as their treatment of Christ Himself. In certain "doctored" Bibles such as one that lies before me now this passage is carefully marked so as to indicate that it does not apply to the "saved" at all. As a translator I wonder by what right the editors of this world-famous tendentious Bible have dared to bracket these incredibly challenging words simply because they do not fit in with their own tight scheme of

[11] Matthew 25:31-46.

salvation. The words were spoken by Christ, and they are plain for all to read, shy as we may be of accepting their implication. They mean that the way we treat other people is a certain indication of the way we treat Christ—indeed, it *is* the way in which we treat Christ. They are revolutionary words and they are meant to be revolutionary. If we follow the way of love, which is the way of Christ, we find ourselves committed not to loving our own little circle but to an attitude of love toward all men. Our aim and our ideal is to be "perfect, even as your Father which is in heaven is perfect." [12] There is a further revolutionary statement from the lips of Christ Himself which shows how closely He links Himself with humanity. Let us read again the parable of the two debtors.[13] If the superevangelists of this world were to take this passage as their text, what far-reaching conversions might follow! For here Jesus declares without the slightest doubt that there is no possibility of God's forgiving us our sins unless we are prepared to forgive sins against our precious selves. How often have I heard evangelists urging penitents to "come to the foot of the Cross," "be washed in the Blood of the Lamb," and so on, yet never once have I heard an evangelist refer, for example, to the words of Jesus which read, "But if ye do not forgive, neither will your Father which is in heaven forgive your trespasses." [14] Yet every time we repeat the prayer which our Lord Himself taught us we ask God to forgive our sins in the same way as we forgive other people who sin against us. I am not in the least attempting to detract from the unique act of Reconciliation which Christ, at infinite cost, made for us on the Cross. Indeed, the very thought of God-become-Man so allowing darkness and evil to close in upon Him and kill Him fills me with awe. But I cannot suppress or minimize the words of that same

[12] Matthew 5:48.   [13] Matthew 18:23–35.   [14] Mark 11:26.

Jesus Christ Who declared categorically, "For if ye forgive men their trespasses, your heavenly Father will also forgive you: but if ye forgive not men their trespasses, neither will your Father forgive your trespasses." [15]

John once asked pertinently, "For he that loveth not his brother whom he hath seen, how can he love God whom he hath not seen?" [16] Of course, if we separate in our minds God and Man, and regard God as wholly Other, the answer is easy. God is unimaginable beauty and goodness; but Man is ignorant, stupid, selfish, and irritating. But if we once digest the truth that God has identified Himself with man in Christ, then we see the force of John's question. We can also realize the force of his bald statement in the same verse, "If a man say, I love God, and hateth his brother, he is a liar." [17] It is unhappily true that quite a number of modern Christians have separated love of God from love of their brothers and sisters. Whenever the Church turns in upon itself and restricts its love to its own members, this fatal split occurs. Whenever the Church turns a blind eye to unfair racial discrimination, or to flagrant snobbery, it is exhibiting exactly the opposite spirit to the spirit of the Incarnation. We may much prefer cut-and-dried schemes of salvation and the comfortable feeling that we are one of the saved, but we may safely infer from the sayings of Jesus that no individual or church finds salvation unless love of God goes hand in hand with love of fellow men.

4. *The temptation to feel that people are not worth loving.* The world is lamentably short of outgoing love. Part of the reason for this is that it is so much easier to love among our own circle or at least to love those who will return our love. Although we do not express it in so

---

[15] Matthew 6:14–15.   [16] 1 John 4:20b.   [17] 1 John 4:20a.

many words, I believe that one of the reasons so few people venture to give themselves for the sake of other people is that they feel that "people are not really worth it." But who are we, we who call ourselves Christians, "saved," pillars of the Church, and so on? In what way do we think that we were "worth it," when Christ visited this earth to save us? In the eyes of Heaven this whole sin-infected, blundering human race could hardly have seemed worthy of the highest sacrifice which God Himself could make for its redemption. Yet Love took the initiative and bore unspeakable contradiction, misunderstanding, and humiliation to win us to Himself. To quote John's words again, "If God so loved us, we ought also to love one another." [18]

This sense of first being loved and then being willing to give oneself in love is the secret of a life such as that of Paul. I mention Paul simply because we know a fair amount about his life, but there must have been hundreds of others whose names we do not even know who gave themselves similarly in love to the world around them; yet how rare is that love found in the Church today among its ordinary members! Thank God there are exceptions in all the Churches, men and women who will go into the dark and messy situations of human life to bring the light and order of Christ! There are at this moment thousands of such people scattered throughout the world—doctors, nurses, pastors, teachers, social workers of all kinds—who make tremendous sacrifices because they are impelled by the love of Christ. But they are a tiny minority compared with the membership figures of all the churches. Why is there, in this country at least, such a tragic shortage of Christian workers? Men and women are desperately needed not only to teach in Sunday school and

[18] 1 John 4:11.

run youth organizations, but to bring the salvation of Christ to the juvenile delinquents, to guide and teach and shepherd in His Name thousands who have no hope and are "without God in the world." [19] As I have traveled about this country the story is almost always the same: "If only we had devoted men and women as Christian leaders . . ." The real lack is the lack of love. Not enough people have realized the Love of God and His tremendous Purpose; not enough have so experienced His Love that they are prepared to love other people at considerable personal cost. There can be no revival of the Church's life or the Church's influence until the love of God sweeps once more into the hearts of men and women as it did into the Young Church.

The Love Deficiency

We have already tried to take an imaginative glance at this planet from the angels' point of view. Probably next to the shriveling of the faith faculty and the closely allied dying down of hope, the most disturbing symptom of the world's disease in the eyes of Heaven is the lack of outgoing love. It is perfectly true, as John pointed out, that "love casts out fear," but it is also horribly true that fear casts out love. In a world full of tensions and anxieties, strife, envy, and suspicion, love and goodwill are very largely driven out. The very best of human schemes fail through sheer lack of love to implement them. Now it should be obvious that if there is to be a fresh intake of love, it can only come from God Himself, and that it can only be received by those who are willing to be open to God and ready to cooperate with His Purpose. To come down to ourselves, our poverty-stricken love can only be

[19] Ephesians 2:12.

enriched and deepened by making ourselves wide open to the love of God. For this cleansing and reinvigorating process we must have deliberate and planned periods of quiet communion with God. There is no other solvent for our prides and prejudices than this love. Fear will not be driven from our hearts by resolution only, but by the willing reception of the very Spirit of Love. A lot of this must, I think, be done in private, but much more must be done in Christian fellowship. To whatever church we belong we must meet together far more frequently than hitherto to receive in faith the Body and Blood of our Lord. This is above all our Appointment with God, the place and the time where Heaven meets the deficiencies of earth. Here, under cover of the earthly and ordinary, we may receive the spiritual and supranatural. There can be no doubt that the Young Church renewed not only its faith and courage but that deep love which went far beyond the emotions of the fellowship itself by meeting together for "the breaking of bread and the prayers." [20] All of us who are spiritually awake at all are conscious of and concerned about the needs of the world around us. I have read the results of much study on the problem of how the ordinary men and women outside the churches may be won for Christ. One conclusion is common to the results of any group or church who have studied and prayed about this problem. It is simply this, that people can only be *loved* into the Kingdom of God. I believe this is profoundly true, and no method or organization, however useful in itself, will compensate for the lack of love. This is where we are driven back upon God, Who is Love. Where else shall we draw our supplies of compassion and self-giving, our willingness to serve? Who else can trans-

[20] Acts 2:42.

form us from people with a limited ability to love into people who can feel real concern for the condition of others who are far outside our natural circles of living? From what other source shall we find the courage to go into unpromising situations and redeem them by the power of love?

"The greatest of these is love," [21] wrote Paul long ago, and we all agree, with admiration. But how far do our lives endorse what we assent to so readily? "The greatest of these is success" might well be the motto of many people, even though they themselves are not successful. "The greatest of these is security" is the motto of countless thousands. "The greatest of these is knowledge" is the unexpressed opinion of many of our scientifically-minded generation. We have to become convinced afresh that Paul's inspired words are quite literally true. Love is the greatest because without it there is no worth-while success and certainly no real security. Love is the greatest because men are never transformed at heart permanently except by love. Love is the greatest because without it knowledge can become dangerous and even suicidal. Above all, love is the greatest because it persists beyond the confines of this temporal existence. The success of the film star, the brilliance of the best selling novelist, the speed of the record-breaking athlete, the awe-inspiring knowledge of the top-secret scientist—of what value will these and a hundred other highly prized worldly achievements amount to in the Real World to which we are bound? But what has been done in love—the problems that have been solved, the personalities redeemed, the situations changed, the actual growth of character beneath the influence of love—all these will stand as permanent and demonstrable evidence

[21] 1 Corinthians 13:13.

of the divine Purpose of Love. All of us are inclined to be swayed more than we realize by the values of the world in which we live, but must we be so dazzled and blinded that we fail to see the paramount importance as well as the permanence of Love?

Peace

Despite the fire, energy, daring, hope, and faith that distinguished the Young Church, there is no trace of hysteria or morbid excitement in its recorded life. Some of us have seen people do all sorts of extraordinary things under the influence of religious excitement, and those of us who are pastors of souls have sometimes been not a little perturbed at the dangers of arousing religious emotions and at their equally dangerous reactions. But as we study New Testament Christianity we are aware that there is an inner core of tranquillity and stability. In fact, not the least of the impressive qualities which the Church could demonstrate to the pagan world was this ballast of inward peace. It was, I think, something new that was appearing in the lives of human beings. It was not mere absence of strife or conflict, and certainly not the absence of what ordinarily makes for anxiety; nor was it a lack of sensitivity or a complacent self-satisfaction, which can often produce an apparent tranquillity of spirit. It was a positive peace, a solid foundation which held fast amid all the turmoil of human experience. It was, in short, the experience of Christ's bequest when He said, "Peace I leave with you, my peace I give unto you: not as the world giveth, give I unto you." [1]

[1] John 14:27.

Although essential human nature has not changed, outward circumstances have changed enormously since the early days of the Christian Faith. I do not think that we can claim that life is either more difficult or more dangerous, but modern living is certainly more complex and is certainly conducted at a higher speed. The natural factors which tend to destroy peace and tranquillity are greater than ever. All the more reason, then, for Christians to experience and, consciously or unconsciously, to show living evidence of the divine gift—of the unshakable inner core of peace.

"Peace with God" is sometimes rather carelessly used in religious circles as though it had only one connotation, as though all the problems of a complex human personality were solved if only a man would accept the redemptive sacrifice of Christ upon the Cross. Actually, this is an oversimplification, for although to accept the reconciliation which God has provided is an absolute essential, there are many other factors, especially among the more intelligent, which prevent the soul from being at peace. The divine peace, the steady centering of life upon God, is basically a gift from God and must be accepted, like our forgiveness, as His gift and not as something that we can achieve. Nevertheless there are elements within our own personalities which must be frankly faced before we can expect to experience that gift. If we want to enjoy inward tranquillity amid this whirling, bewildering modern life, we must be prepared to do some honest self-examination. In the last resort we shall find that our only true peace is "peace with God," but it may not prove quite so simple to find it as we imagined. Let us consider some of the factors which prevent us from enjoying inner peace, and how we may cope with them.

1. *The problem of self-pleasing.* In all of us, to a greater or less degree, depending on heredity, upbringing, and temperament, there is a thrusting, self-pleasing element which normally regards the world as centering upon oneself. It is not a thing to be horrified at, for it is in us all, but the whole way of thinking and feeling which belongs to the self-centered man must be abrogated or denied before there can be peace with God. What we call "sins" are simply expressions of this self-pleasing, self-regarding, and self-indulgent inward attitude. The word which is translated in the New Testament as "repentance" really means a thorough change of heart and mind. It means realizing that the real center of everything is not my little self, but God, and that in order to serve the King Himself I must quit the throne of my own precious little kingdom. To some people this comes easily, almost naturally, as soon as they see the truth of it. To others it means a hard and even agonizing struggle. Such people do not readily surrender; they do not easily cooperate with someone else's plan, even if that Someone Else is God. Yet it is obvious that there can be no inward peace until the self-conscious inward kingdom willingly and wholeheartedly concedes its rights to the Creator, the real King.

This is the essential of all Christian living, but in actual experience it does not happen all at once. A man may not realize how strong and deeply entrenched is his own self-interest until he has followed Christ even for years. It is the willing cooperation that God is seeking, the cheerful enlisting in His service. Certain types of people can be scared into being "saved" or "converted," but it does not necessarily follow that they willingly hand over the center of their being to the service of Christ. As far as we can judge from the New Testament, people are not frightened into becoming Christians. Jesus required His followers to be "fishers of men," and the ability to instill fear is not a prime qualification for a fisherman! In the classic instance of sudden conversion, that is, of Paul, it is interesting to note that there is no threat of hell-fire, not even of reproach in the words Jesus spoke to him in the vision on the Damascus road.[2] We might well have thought that the man who had been responsible for the death, disgrace, misery, and imprisonment of so many of Christ's men and women would naturally have incurred the wrath of the Lord Himself. But what do we find? A penetrating question, asking in effect, "Why are you behaving like this toward Me?" and a highly significant comment, "It is not easy for you to go against your own conscience."[3] Paul saw in a blinding moment of revelation how the whole structure of his righteous living, including his violent persecutions of the truth, had been utterly self-centered. What is more, he saw the Lord personally, and the consequence of seeing himself as he was and Christ as He was resulted in a thoroughgoing conversion. Such complete visions of the truth are rare. But it is as this same truth strikes home to men by the power of the Spirit that they realize the true position—how off course they are, what harm their self-centered living has caused, and how they can only be at peace if they are reconciled with the Nature and Purpose of God.

2. *The resolving of inner conflicts.* If we are quiet before God and allow His Spirit to shine upon our inward state, we shall probably discover more than one conflict which is robbing us of inner peace. The man who lives apart from God may be largely unconscious of his inward conflicts and only aware of their tension. Of course, he

[2] Acts 9.   [3] Acts 9:4–5.

may be driven by the sheer force of the tension to a psychiatrist who, if he is a wise one, will help the man to realize the sources of his disharmony. But he still will not be at peace with the Nature of things, with his own conscience and the Divine Purpose that is being worked out in this world, unless the psychiatrist is able to lead him to faith in God. But except in unusual cases the Christian need not turn to the psychiatrist. Either alone with God or with the help of a trusted friend, priest, or minister, he can, if he wishes, see for himself the fierce hidden resentment, the carefully concealed self-importance, the obstinate and unforgiving spirit, and all the other things which prevent inward relaxation. As long as his personality is a battleground it is foolish to suggest to him that he accepts the peace of God. His hidden desires, ambitions, and prides must first be brought to the surface, not only to the surface of his own consciousness but, as it were, to the light of God's love and understanding. God is not concerned to condemn; however ashamed and guilty the man himself may feel, God is concerned to heal and to harmonize.

3. *The sharing of life with God.* For sheer practical wisdom Paul's famous words have never been surpassed. He wrote: "Be careful for nothing; but in every thing by prayer and supplication with thanksgiving let your requests be made known unto God. And the peace of God, which passeth all understanding, shall keep your hearts and minds through Christ Jesus." [4] It is when the love of God is allowed to penetrate every corner of a man's being that the peace of God comes as a positive gift, as a sturdy guardian of the soul's inward rest. The sharing of anxieties and fears, the intimate thankfulness for joys and beauties,

[4] Philippians 4:6–7.

bring the individual very close to the life of God. They must be habitual and they must be practiced, but their fruit is a relaxed spirit.

4. *Realization of adequate resources.* Much of our tension and anxiety can be traced directly to a fear of inadequacy. We should meet this fear in two ways. First, by learning to accept ourselves. We probably are *not* adequate for all our ambitious schemes, and only at the cost of enormous nervous energy can we succeed in becoming momentarily what we really are not. This is a self-imposed tyranny which is very common. Suppose we accept ourselves good-humoredly, realizing our limitations and how much we have to learn, with cheerfulness and without envy of those who are, or appear to be, more adequate than ourselves. It is simply no use at all claiming the gift of God's peace if we are ridden by an overmastering desire to appear bigger or cleverer or more important than we really are. We must first learn to practice acceptance. The second step is to learn to accept life, as Jesus Himself did, at the Father's hands *day by day*. It was not a cynic but the Son of God Himself Who said, "One day's trouble is enough for one day." [5] We are assured by many inspired promises that God will give us, as we require it, the ability to cope with life victoriously on this day-by-day basis. We must teach ourselves to get out of the habit of thinking too far ahead, of imagining ourselves tomorrow or next week as inadequate for a situation which exists only in our minds. The sooner we can get it into our feverish souls that we are meant to live a day at a time, the more we shall be able to enjoy that sense of adequacy which spells peace of mind.

[5] Matthew 6:34b.

5. *Peace as a positive gift.* I have mentioned above only a few of the psychological factors which may prevent us from enjoying the peace of God. To some simple natures it will appear as though I have overcomplicated the issue. But it is the fortunate few whose inward growth and life is so simple (and by that of course I do not mean stupid) that they can quite readily accept in unquestioning faith the peace of God within their hearts. To others it will naturally appear that I have done no more than touch upon their difficulties, which indeed is all that I have done. I can only recommend here that there must be a full, unashamed bringing to the surface of all the warring elements within the personality. In making such unravelings and adjustments as we can, we are not creating peace; we are only creating conditions for the coming of peace. When our hearts are possessed by this gift of God, we know for certain how true it is that it "passeth man's understanding." Outward circumstances may be tempestuous; common sense may tell us that it is absurd to be at peace under such a load or such a threat. But the gift is supranatural; it goes far beyond earthly common sense. It is, like faith, hope, and love, rooted in the Purpose of God.

6. *Alignment with the Purpose.* Peace with God is not a static emotion. It is a positive gift which accompanies our living in harmony with God's Plan. Dante's oft quoted saying, "And in His will is our peace," is not to be understood as surrender, resignation, and quiescence. The Christian will discover that he knows God's peace as he is aligned with God's Purpose. He may be called upon to be strenuous, but he is inwardly relaxed because he knows he is doing the Will of God. This sense of knowing that he is cooperating with the Purpose defies human analysis and

is always found singularly irritating by the opponent of Christianity. But Christians of all ages, not excepting our own, have found it to be true. However painful or difficult or, on the other hand, however inconspicuous or humdrum the life may be, the Christian finds his peace in accepting and playing his part in the Master Plan. Here again we must ask ourselves, "Am I doing what God wants me to do?" It is not a question of what my friends or a particular Christian pressure group want me to do, but of what God Himself wishes. By sharing our life with God, by throwing open our personality to His love and wisdom, we can know beyond any doubting what is God's will for us. When we are at one with Him in spirit and at one with Him in purpose, we may know the deep satisfaction of the peace of God.

Christian Maintenance

In order to live a life of New Testament quality we shall find it necessary to work out some kind of practical plan to keep us alive and sensitive to the Spirit of the living God, which will keep us supplied day by day with the necessary spiritual reinforcement, and which will help us to grow and develop as sons and daughters of God. It is unfortunately only too easy to slip back into conformity with our immediate surroundings and to lose sight of the suprahuman way of living, except perhaps as a wistful memory. This does not in the least mean that real Christian living is a kind of spiritual tightrope walk, a fantastic and unnatural progress which can only be maintained by intense concentration. On the contrary, the Christian way of living is *real* living, and it carries all the satisfaction and exhilaration which living in reality can bring. It is quite simply because we are surrounded by unreal and false values, by a pattern of living divorced from and unconscious of spiritual realities, that we have to take time and trouble to maintain supranatural life, even though that life is in the truest sense the natural one. Experience shows that Christians whose lives are illuminated by the new quality of living only maintain that inner radiance by taking certain practical steps. Naturally these will vary in individual cases, and there are people who, either by tem-

perament or through long years of practice, can absorb
God through the pores of their being, so to speak, as
naturally and easily as most of us can breathe. But for the
majority of us who are walking "by faith and not by
sight" there are some essentials for the maintenance of
real Christian living.

The first essential need is for quiet. The higher the
function of the human spirit, the more necessity for quiet-
ness. We cannot, for example, solve a difficult mathe-
matical problem, neither can we appreciate good music,
nor indeed art in any form, if we are surrounded by noisy
distractions. It is imperative that somehow or other we
make for ourselves a period of quiet each day. I know how
difficult this is for many people in busy households, and
for some even the bedroom is not quiet or private enough.
But if we see the utter necessity for this period of quiet
our ingenuity will find a way of securing it. Many churches
are open for this purpose among others, and there is no
reason at all why we should not use the quiet of the reading room of the Public Library. But daily quiet we simply
must secure, or the noise and pressure of modern life will
quickly smother our longing to live life of the new quality.

What we must do in the period of quiet is to open
our lives to God—to perfect understanding, wisdom and
love. Perhaps it seems unnecessary to point this out, yet
pastoral experience convinces me that people need to be
reminded that we must be completely natural and unin-
hibited in our approach to the God "in whom we live
and move and have our being." Most practicing Christians
have got beyond feeling that God must be addressed in
Elizabethan English in deference to His Majesty, but
there still lingers on an idea that we must be spiritually
"dressed in our best" as we approach Him. I am far from
suggesting that we should ever treat the awe-inspiring mys-

tery of God with overfamiliarity. Yet we know perfectly well, on the authority of Christ, that He is our heavenly Father, and our common sense tells us that, although He respects our individuality and our privacy, yet everything about us is quite open to His eyes. We are not addressing some superearthly King, some magnified Boss; we are not even addressing a purified and enlarged image of our own earthly fathers. We are opening our hearts and minds to Love, and we need have no fears, no reticences, and no pretenses. Strange as it undoubtedly is, He loves us as we are, and indeed we shall make no sort of progress unless we approach Him as we are.

Prayer has so many aspects that it requires much longer treatment than I can give it here, and I will only mention three which seem to me the most important. The first is the value of worship. For myself I do not think worship can be forced, nor can I imagine that God wants it so to be. But if we make a habit of associating all that is good, true, lovely, and heartwarming in our ordinary experience of life and people with Him Who is the Source of every good and perfect gift; if without forcing ourselves to be grateful we quietly recount those things for which we can be truly thankful; if we allow our own dreams and aspirations to lead us upward to the One from Whom they are in fact derived, we shall not infrequently find that the springs of worship begin to flow. Sometimes a consideration of the Character of Christ as revealed in the Gospels, sometimes a consideration of the whole vast Plan for man's redemption, and sometimes a consideration of the immense complexity and wisdom revealed in a dozen different departments by the researches of Science will move us to wonder, admiration, awe, and worship.

The second important point I should like to make is that in our prayers we should not merely confess our sins and failures to God, but claim from Him the opposite virtue. If we stress again and again our own particular failings, we tend to accentuate and even to perpetuate them. Many of us Christians need to adopt a more positive attitude. We need to dare to draw upon the inexhaustible riches of Christ, not as though that were some poetic and metaphorical expression, but as though it were a fact. The Gospel is not Good News if it simply underlines our own sinfulness. That is either a foregone conclusion or it is Bad News! But the whole wonder and glory of the Gospel is that into people who have sinned and failed badly God can pour not only the healing of forgiveness but the positive reactivating power of goodness. It is not the mere overcoming of a fault that we should seek from God, but such an overflowing gift of the opposite virtue that we are transformed. I cannot believe that the miracles of personality transformation, which undoubtedly occurred in such places as Corinth and Ephesus nineteen centuries ago, are beyond the power of God's activity today. We are altogether too timorous and tentative. Why should we not make bold and far-reaching demands upon the spiritual riches which are placed at our disposal?

Thirdly, I should like to stress the value of intercession for other people. I do not pretend to understand the mystery of intercession, though I am sure it is never an attempt to bend the will of a reluctant God to do something good in other people's lives. But somehow in the mysterious spiritual economy in which we live we are required to give love, sympathy, and understanding in our prayers for others, and this releases God's power of love in ways and at depths which would otherwise prove beyond our reach. I confess I stand amazed at the power of intercessory prayer, and not least at what I can only call the "celestial ingenuity" of God. He does not, as a rule, directly intervene;

He assaults no man's personality, and He never interferes with the free will which He has given to men. Yet, working within these apparently paralyzing limitations, God's love, wisdom, and power are released and become operative in response to faithful intercessory prayer. It is all part of the high Purpose, and all true Christians are responsibly involved in such praying.

It is very noticeable in the New Testament records of the early Church that Christianity existed in fellowship. Of course, it may easily be pointed out that a sect which was such a tiny minority in a pagan world would be forced to close its ranks and stand together if it were to survive at all. That is perfectly true, but it was surely more than mere expediency that kept the early Christians together. Surely part of their extraordinary strength and vitality was due to their being "of one heart and mind." They worshiped and prayed together; they shared in "the breaking of bread." [1] Even though, judging from the evidence of Paul's letters, it was not very long before factions and "splinter groups" arose, yet the over-all picture is of the Young Church standing firm and fearless in fellowship.

Because human beings are for the most part gregarious by nature, they tend to join with others who have similar interests. There are clubs, associations, fraternities, and societies without number throughout the whole civilized world to join together in fellowship people whose common interest may be fly fishing, stamp collecting, bird watching, hiking, photography, gardening, interplanetary travel, or any of a host of widely assorted subjects. Since this is so, it would appear to the casual observer that the fellowship of the Church is simply another organization, in this case an association of people whose interests lie in the Christian religion. But this is very far from being the case,

[1] Acts 2:42.

for the fellowship of Christians is the outward manifesta-
tion of a deep spiritual unity. Men and women have discovered through the living Spirit of God what they are
meant to be and the Plan with which they are called to
cooperate. They have discovered the reality of the spiritual
order and, what is even more important, they have found
that Jesus Christ is no mere Figure of history but a
living contemporary Person Whose personality and power
cleanses and invigorates their own. They have discovered
beneath the surface of different temperaments and back-
grounds that they belong to the same family—that they
are all sons and daughters of the same Father. They are, in
a world largely insensitive to the true order of things,
"picked representatives" of the new humanity.[2] In a very
real sense they are carrying on the work which Christ began
so long ago, not so much in admiration and memory of
Him, but as people dedicated to follow the leading of His
contemporary Spirit. They form together, as Paul pointed
out long ago, "the body of Christ." [3] They are not a human organization but a suprahuman organism. They are
the life of the real world being expressed in human terms
in the present temporary setup.

Of course, all the above may appear a pathetically or
even a ridiculously idealistic picture of the modern Church.
But surely the words fairly represent what the Church
should be and could be, and they at least partly explain
why Christian fellowship in the Church is far more essential than any human association for the promotion of
this, that, or the other. Because Christians are "members
one of another" they must work as an organic whole,
different as their individual functions may be. All this
means that a very large part of our Christian maintenance
will consist of joining in with the fellowship of the Church,

[2] Colossians 3:12.   [3] 1 Corinthians 12:27.

in its prayer and worship, in its work and service. Many people who profess to be Christians are very irregular worshipers. I do not think they can possibly realize how they weaken the cause of the Church and in addition starve themselves of Christian fellowship. Many people appear to be convinced that they can lead good lives without committing themselves to Church attendance or the fellowship of the Church. Of course, if the object of Christianity were to produce good respectable people quite a fair proportion could go on being good and respectable and even bringing up good and respectable children without much aid from the Church. But suppose that is not the point at all; it certainly is not the point in the New Testament. The Church is never regarded as a rallying ground for the good and respectable. On the contrary it is a fellowship of those whose lives have been transformed by Christ, a fellowship of those who have become aware of the vast spiritual struggle which is taking place on the stage of this planet, a fellowship of those who are the actual living instruments of God's Purpose today. If our aim is merely morality we may very well be able to do without the Church, but if we are being called as sons and daughters of God to cooperate with His high Purpose in the redemption of mankind, we cannot absent ourselves from the fellowship of other Christians without greatly impoverishing both that fellowship and our own souls. If you had stood, as I have stood for so many years, in the shoes of a minister of religion, you would see the situation with very different eyes. You would see, as the parson does, that when it is an extra fine day and you say, "I think I will give the Christian fellowship a miss today; let us get out into the country," thousands of others say and do exactly the same thing. The result is not merely that public worship is thinly attended, but we miss more than it is possible to estimate the corporate prayer and the renewal week by week of our common dedication to our unseen Lord. Yes, and on the purely human level we miss the mutual encouragement and warmth that only a full Church fellowship can bring.

Again, if the Church is to make any worth-while impact on the surrounding community, if it is even to speak with a voice worth hearing, it must have the active, committed support of all true Christians. I repeat, I do not think that the many delightful casual Christians whom I know have the slightest idea how they sabotage the power and witness of the Christian fellowship by their haphazard attachment to the Church. Now, we have already admitted that the early Church was compelled to be a close-knit fellowship in order to survive against all the forces of paganism. The forces of paganism are no less powerful today, although they are not nearly so obviously dangerous. Modern materialism, secularism, abysmal ignorance about God and His Plan for life are very real enemies on the side of darkness, and the lone Christian does less than nothing for the army of light when he remarks, "I find I can be just as good a Christian without ever joining the Church."

This whole question of entering fully into the worship and work of the Church must be faced by all those who genuinely desire to serve Christ in this modern age. There is an immense amount of diffused goodwill and willingness to serve others in countries with a Christian tradition such as this. Such things are far from valueless to the community as a whole, but I am convinced they would be far more potent in coping with mankind's ills and necessities if they were part of the extramural work of the Church of Christ. The Christian Church should surely be the center of inspiration, as well as the meeting place for worship and prayer, for all those who are dealing with man's difficult problems, quite frequently in an unconsciously Christian spirit. But as long as even professing Christians refrain from giving their wholehearted loyalty to the Church, it is not surprising that the vast number of unconscious Christians fail to see the point of joining a fellowship so poorly supported. In my own opinion, and speaking only for this country, a revival of true religion and a recovery of spiritual values could quite easily begin if the existing Churches were fully supported by their present members. These men and women of goodwill, quite a number of whom I know personally, who are giving such wonderful selfless service to their fellows, might see in an alert and vital Church the true center of their own aspirations and endeavors. They might see the point of bringing their own gifts, skill, and experience into a sincerely committed fellowship, and both they and the Church would be immeasurably enriched by such a step. But so long as professing Christians remain so loosely attached to their Church, there is not likely to be a core, a deep spiritual fellowship, which could attract the man who is serving humanity in a Christian spirit without knowing exactly why.

Sharing our inward lives then, and joining in the fellowship, worship, and service of the Church are essentials for Christian maintenance. Very close to them in importance lies the habit of regular Bible reading. Countless men and women throughout the centuries have found their inspiration and nourishment for the Christian life in reading the Word of God. Now, I am not at all sure that our modern way of living is suited to the old-fashioned methods of Bible study. It is not really going to help us to live today if we know, for example, the chronological order of the kings of Israel and Judah, or study verse by verse the book of Lamentations or the book of Esther. If we are pressed for time, and most of us are, what we chiefly need to do is to study the four Gospels and soak ourselves in their spirit, and then to study with imagination the Epistles or Letters, which reflect the life of the vigorous Young Church. I am far from writing off the Old Testament as useless; but to the modern follower of Christ, whose time is limited, it is infinitely more important that he should know intimately the four recorded lives of Christ and the message of the letters of the New Testament than to possess cover-to-cover knowledge of the whole Bible, which is bound to be sketchy and superficial. To my mind the day of "proof texts" is over. It is not a matter of guiding our life and conduct by finding a particular verse or phrase. What is important is that we should really understand to the limit of our ability what sort of Person Christ was, what were His methods, and what were His aims. We need to know what He did in fact say about the important questions affecting life and death, which all of us have to face sooner or later. We need to use our minds, to be as unfettered as we possibly can be from prejudice and religious indoctrination. Let us see and feel for ourselves what Christ really was and really taught. Let us allow our minds and spirits to be thoroughly influenced, not by the traditions of men, but by what Christ Himself was, said, and taught. He is "the same yesterday, and to-day, and for ever," [4] and as we read His recorded life we can reflect that it is not fancy but sober fact that He Himself stands beside us to guide and instruct us. We need His living Spirit to make the connection between the world of New Testament days and the world in which we have to live today.

This intelligent reading, particularly of the New Testament, will keep alive and alert our inmost spirits. The

[4] Hebrews 13:8.

sacred pages are truly inspired, not I believe in any "verbal inspirational" sense, but because they contain the Word of God or, in case that is a meaningless cliché, they contain truths of the Real World in the language of this. Again and again we shall find ourselves challenged, convicted, inspired, or comforted by truths that are not of man's making at all, but which are bright shafts of light breaking through into our darkness.

Closely allied to intelligent Bible study lies Christian reading. It is a profound mistake to suppose that the Holy Spirit of God ceased to inspire writers when the New Testament had been completed. There are many Christians today who from one year's end to another never read a Christian book. They have little or no idea, for example, how Christianity is spreading throughout the world, of the triumphs and disappointments of the world-wide Church. They have given themselves no chance to know why there is a world-wide movement toward a once more united Church. They do not know the Christian answer to the challenge of Communism; they are even hazy about the very real and solid achievements of Christian men and women throughout the centuries. To be brutally frank, they are very ignorant both of the history and of the implications of their Faith. In other departments of life they may be highly competent, efficient, and knowledgeable, but over this, the very heart and center of their true life, they are frequently abysmally ignorant. These are, I know, harsh words; but the Church could be infinitely more powerful as God's instrument for the establishment of His Kingdom if its members were better informed in their minds as well as more devoted in their hearts.

Christian Service

The early vigorous Church was essentially a working, serving, and forward-looking Church. Partly because of a sensitivity to the Spirit's direction and partly because of the rising tide of persecution the Young Church did not have much chance of becoming self-satisfied and complacent. It expanded and spread into all sorts of unlikely places armed only with the Good News of the love and power of the Spirit. Throughout the New Testament letters we can see how insistent are Paul and the others that the love of God which has sprung up in men's hearts at the touch of Christ must be expressed in outward conduct toward a pagan and frequently hostile world. The early Christians were pioneers of a new way of life, and many of them plainly regarded themselves as expendable for the cause of the Kingdom. The time had not yet come for any church to become inward-looking, prosperous, or self-satisfied.

Sometimes nowadays one gets the impression that the Christian churches have largely ceased to look outward. It is almost as though Christians exist in a closed circle of fellowship, with all their members facing inward, while behind their backs there are the millions who long, albeit unconsciously, for the Gospel, and for the point and purpose in life that only the Gospel can bring. If the churches are to recover the vast power and influence of the Church of New Testament times, there must be a fundamental change of attitude in many churches, which means, of course, a fundamental change in the attitude of the churches' members. We must recover our sense of vocation, our sense that we are not, as I said above, an organization of people who have a common interest in religion, but the local representatives of the God Whom we serve and of the Heaven to which we belong.

We may be full of joy, but we are not here for our own amusement. We are here to be used as instruments in God's Purpose. It is a fine thing to know that we are "right with God," "converted," "born again," and all the rest of it, but after a while such experiences become stale and unsatisfying unless we are passing the Good News on to others, positively assisting the work of the Church, or definitely bringing to bear upon actual human situations the pattern of Christian living. This means in effect that each Christian must ask himself, "Am I myself outward-looking in my Christian experience, or am I content to remain in a safe 'Christian rut'?" The recovery of the Church's power rests ultimately upon the individual Christian's answer to such a question.

Coming down to actual practice, the Christian has to ask himself what he can do to express outwardly and effectively his inward spiritual certainty. Obviously his first duty is to live a Christian life in his home and in his place of work. This is where his witness is most effective, and frequently most difficult, but busy-ness in Church affairs is no substitute whatever for exhibiting Christian graces in the home or being known as a Christian in our place of work. But, assuming that we have seriously considered our ordinary Christian life and witness, we ought also as members of the Church to think seriously of what our contribution should be in terms of time, personality, and talent to the life of the church to which we belong. I have already referred to the horrifying paucity of *leaders* in most of our churches, of men and women who will take responsibility and work at a job for the love of Christ and His Church. The influence of the Christian fellowship upon children, upon adolescents, upon the community in which the Church's life is set would be vastly enhanced if even half the existing church members were to give a single hour of dedicated service every week to their church. Of course, to do such a thing even at the one-hour-per-week rate is costly, and a hundred different excuses crowd readily into the mind. But if the Church is to revive and become once more ablaze with the truth of God and full of the warmth of His love, its members must be prepared to meet the cost and make the sacrifice. The by-product will be of course the maintenance of a high level in the spiritual life of the individual members. For the real danger to professing Christians lies not in the more glaring and grosser temptations and sins, but in a slow deterioration of vision, a slow death to daring, courage, and the willingness to adventure.

I cannot refrain from bringing this to a personal point. Our gifts vary enormously; we cannot all be evangelists, pastors, or teachers. We cannot all be leaders or bear great responsibility, but there is certain to be something, some worth-while piece of service, which only you the reader can do. It may be exciting, it may be humdrum, it may be participating in a new venture, or it may be a mere routine. The apparent importance of it does not really matter; what is of real consequence both to your church and to your own soul is whether you are willing to give yourself sacrificially.

Some Conclusions

The foregoing chapters have all been given as addresses to groups of people in different parts of England and in California, and naturally they have been followed by discussion. Speaking generally, I find a widespread desire to recapture the power and energy of the newborn Church and a very marked willingness, particularly among young people, to give themselves sacrificially to the service of Christ. I have learned a great deal from these frank and free discussions and I have reached the following conclusions.

1. The way of recovery for modern man lies undoubtedly through the recovery of the whole Christian Church. Throughout the centuries there has been no deep and lasting revitalization of the Christian religion unless the rekindled faith has been welded into the life of the existing Church. Enthusiastic "splinter groups" and separatist movements may blaze impressively for a time, but if the new life is to be effectual it must flow into the body of believers already existing, however moribund and defeated they may appear to have become. It is not so much the isolated Christian as a purified and refreshed fellowship which will be the effective witness to a largely despairing world.

2. I find that there is a definite movement toward a

101

united Church and a very deep desire to see the end of
"our unhappy divisions." I have found this strongly
marked desire in all denominations, including my own,
and for myself I would say that unless a man is completely
blind and bigoted he could scarcely deny that the living
Spirit of God is using gentle but considerable pressures to
bring all Christians together. Young Christians particularly, many of whom are in daily contact in office, garage,
factory, and workshop with ardent young Communists,
find the tragedy of a divided Christendom a painful ob-
stacle to their witness. As has been brought home to me
so many times, the points of agreement among the Christian denominations are so very much larger than the points
of disagreement that, surrounded as we are by a largely
pagan world, it is the height of folly to say or do anything
which postpones the process of unity or perpetuates our
differences. Prayer is probably the best weapon here, since
a real influx of the living Spirit into existing denominations would quickly expose the stupidity and sin of maintaining denominational barriers of which, be it firmly said,
many keen young Christians are not even aware.

3. I am not at all convinced that the modern evange-
listic techniques of arousing sin and guilt are the best. The
successes of such campaigns are paraded before us, but in
common with many other clergy and ministers I know
something of the failures. I know of scores of people who
are naturally resistant to guilt injection but who would, I
believe, be among the first to follow Christ, if they could
only see Him. But they are not going to be shouted at or
crooned over, and they give mass meetings a wide berth. I
believe that, although of course we are all "sinners," the
clamant modern need is to be "saved" from the materialism and hopelessness of modern civilization rather than
from the sins the evangelist denounces. Most people in

my experience are not so much sinful as bewildered. They need to be shown Christ as He really is. They need to be shown in fresh ways the basic Christian belief that God, Who is far greater and more complex in His wisdom than our grandfathers ever imagined, became focused for our understanding as well as for our salvation in the Man Jesus. They need to be shown afresh the vast scheme of the redemption of human living, the building of the Kingdom of God. They need to be shown the new quality of living available through the living Spirit of Christ. They need to be shown the spiritual "dimension"—that this little life is only part of a vast scheme which God Himself is working out. As far as I can see they will not become aware of any of these things by having their sins thunderously denounced. It is not the sentimental "Jesus" of the religious crooner that they need, but the living Christ. When they see Him, when they attempt to follow Him, they will find soon enough, as we all do, that there is much in their lives to be forgiven, and that without the Spirit the new life remains an unattainable ideal. They will find, in short, that they are "sinners." But I am quite certain that it is a profound mistake psychologically, spiritually, and in every other sort of way to begin by telling people about their sins, and I would to God that modern evangelists would study the technique of Christ Himself in dealing with actual human personalities.

All the above, and a great deal more, needs to be thought out with the utmost care. We must studiously avoid the cliché and the overused familiar phrase which are meaningless to the man who is outside the Church. We need to reword, to retranslate, as it were, the Good News. We need so to present the Character and Purpose of God that men and women will seek in it not so much individual salvation (though that is included), but a worth-while Cause with which people will joyfully cooperate and to which they will willingly give their adult loyalty.

4. Closely allied to the problem of presenting the Good News in relevant, attention-compelling terms is the need to enlist in the service of Christ's Church the diffused goodwill of the vast army of "unconscious Christians." Again, as far as I can see, the technique of modern high-pressure evangelists has little to offer to such people. I know a number of them personally, and they are already, for reasons of which they are largely unconscious, undeniably exhibiting the fruits of the Spirit. What I am sure they need to be told is that the very ideals which they follow so devotedly derive from an actual Person Who is alive today. How enormously enriched would the life of the Church become if she could receive within her fellowship not merely a small proportion but all the social workers, nurses, doctors, almoners, probation officers, all those who care for the blind, the deaf and dumb, the crippled children, the mentally defective, and the insane! And how fortified and reinspired would so many of these wonderful people be if they were doing their work not merely in obedience to a vague ideal, but for the love of Christ and in the fellowship of His Church!

5. Near the beginning of this book there is a little fantasy called "The Angels' Point of View." I am sure that it would do us all a power of good if we would take time off and use our imaginations to see what is really happening on this earth from the point of view of Heaven. We might see how pathetically ready man is to be fascinated by what we might call the technical marvels of the age, how thrilled he is with the so-called electronic "brain," with the breaking of speed records, by the possibility of an artificial satellite and such-like achievements. Yet if we

were observing life from the true point of view, we should see how infinitely more important it is to recognize what is really going on in the world of human beings than to goggle at any number of physical marvels. We should see, how few, how tragically few, are even trying to find out what the Creator's Plan might be for this world, and how even fewer are prepared to cooperate with it. From the angels' point of view what enormous waste of energy, courage, talent, and personality there must be in many of Man's highly lauded projects! The angels might well ask themselves, "Why does he want to go so fast, to climb so high, to dive so deep, and to complicate his life with so many inventions while he leaves the heart of the matter untouched?" For since Man has been promised a share in the timeless life of God, how blind and earthbound he must appear as he spends his best ingenuities, his highest intellects, and the bulk of his resources upon what is merely ephemeral! If a thousandth part of the devotion and energy which are so freely given to athletic achievement or scientific research were devoted to the building of the Kingdom of God, to better understanding between people, to the production of true brotherhood between nations, what vast forward strides Man, as a potential son of God, could make! But, alas, he can plainly be seen by the angels to be, consciously or unconsciously, avoiding the real issues, where the personal cost is likely to be high. It is infinitely easier and more attractive to plan to visit the moon than to deal with the problem of the juvenile delinquent or the chronic alcoholic. The fun and games grow infinitely more exciting as knowledge increases, but that is hardly an excuse for diverting our best talents and personalities from the real, the spiritual conflict in which our little lives are set.

But because Man's faith faculty is atrophied, and because his knowledge of spiritual resources is infinitesimal, he devotes enormous energies and ingenuity to amassing knowledge and solving problems on their purely physical level. Where the human shoe really pinches, where the problems are moral, psychological, and spiritual, where in fact the painful, patient building of the Kingdom of God is involved, most of our best intellects and personalities are conspicuous by their absence. If it should be a matter of forming an expedition to climb a high mountain range, to explore and survey an unknown territory, or to observe the habits of an almost extinct animal species, volunteers would step forward by the thousand. But when it is a question of dealing at first hand with real human problems, with maladjustment of personality, with malnutrition or illiteracy, with ignorance and superstition—in fact, where it is a matter of entering bravely into human darkness—how few are prepared to volunteer to carry the Light!

If we will train ourselves to see life steadily from the true point of view, we cannot help seeing how very slowly it dawns upon modern man that his real problems, his real conflicts, can never be resolved on the physical plane. A man may travel far faster than sound, but that does not help him in the least to deal with the problem of his own marriage, which is fast breaking up. He may successfully launch an artificial satellite, but that does nothing to solve the squalid conditions in which his fellow men have to live only a few streets away. He may invent and produce commercially 3-D television for every home, but he has not made the slightest contribution toward solving the problems that arise in home, industry, and nation—the selfishness, cruelty, and greed, the fears, resentments, and suspicions that poison our common life. Perhaps the time is not too distant when the bankruptcy of scientific achievement to solve human problems will become increasingly obvious. Perhaps Man will then return, not indeed to rediscover any old-fashioned "hell-fire" religion, but to seek realistically that quality of living which transforms personality, and which we may fairly call New Testament Christianity.